Verses Popular and H

Henry Lawson

Alpha Editions

This edition published in 2024

ISBN : 9789362920041

Design and Setting By
Alpha Editions
www.alphaedis.com
Email - info@alphaedis.com

As per information held with us this book is in Public Domain.
This book is a reproduction of an important historical work. Alpha Editions uses the best technology to reproduce historical work in the same manner it was first published to preserve its original nature. Any marks or number seen are left intentionally to preserve its true form.

Contents

PREFACE .... - 1 -
THE PORTS OF THE OPEN SEA .... - 2 -
THE THREE KINGS[A] .... - 4 -
THE OUTSIDE TRACK .... - 5 -
SYDNEY-SIDE .... - 7 -
THE ROVERS .... - 8 -
FOREIGN LANDS .... - 11 -
MARY LEMAINE .... - 13 -
THE SHAKEDOWN ON THE FLOOR .... - 15 -
REEDY RIVER .... - 17 -
OLD STONE CHIMNEY .... - 19 -
SONG OF THE OLD BULLOCK-DRIVER .... - 22 -
THE LIGHTS OF COBB AND CO. .... - 24 -
HOW THE LAND WAS WON .... - 26 -
THE BOSS OVER THE BOARD .... - 28 -
WHEN THE LADIES COME TO THE SHEARING SHED .. - 30 -
THE BALLAD OF THE ROUSEABOUT .... - 32 -
YEARS AFTER THE WAR IN AUSTRALIA .... - 34 -
THE OLD JIMMY WOODSER .... - 37 -
THE CHRIST OF THE 'NEVER' .... - 38 -
THE CATTLE-DOG'S DEATH .... - 39 -
THE SONG OF THE DARLING RIVER .... - 41 -
RAIN IN THE MOUNTAINS .... - 43 -
A MAY NIGHT ON THE MOUNTAINS .... - 44 -
THE NEW CHUM JACKAROO .... - 45 -
THE DONS OF SPAIN .... - 47 -

THE BURSTING OF THE BOOM	- 48 -
ANTONY VILLA A Ballad of Ninety-three	- 50 -
SECOND CLASS WAIT HERE	- 53 -
THE SHIPS THAT WON'T GO DOWN	- 54 -
THE MEN WE MIGHT HAVE BEEN	- 55 -
THE WAY OF THE WORLD	- 56 -
THE BATTLING DAYS	- 57 -
WRITTEN AFTERWARDS	- 59 -
THE UNCULTURED RHYMER TO HIS CULTURED CRITICS	- 61 -
THE WRITER'S DREAM	- 63 -
THE JOLLY DEAD MARCH	- 66 -
MY LITERARY FRIEND	- 68 -
MARY CALLED HIM 'MISTER'	- 69 -
REJECTED	- 70 -
O'HARA, J.P.	- 72 -
BILL AND JIM FALL OUT	- 75 -
THE PAROO	- 76 -
THE GREEN-HAND ROUSEABOUT	- 78 -
THE MAN FROM WATERLOO (With kind regards to "Banjo.")	- 80 -
SAINT PETER	- 82 -
THE STRANGER'S FRIEND	- 84 -
THE GOD-FORGOTTEN ELECTION	- 86 -
THE BOSS'S BOOTS	- 88 -
THE CAPTAIN OF THE PUSH	- 90 -
BILLY'S 'SQUARE AFFAIR'	- 92 -
A DERRY ON A COVE	- 94 -
RISE YE! RISE YE!	- 95 -

THE BALLAD OF MABEL CLARE	- 96 -
CONSTABLE M'CARTY'S INVESTIGATIONS	- 100 -
AT THE TUG-OF-WAR	- 103 -
HERE'S LUCK!	- 104 -
THE MEN WHO COME BEHIND	- 105 -
THE DAYS WHEN WE WENT SWIMMING	- 106 -
THE OLD BARK SCHOOL	- 108 -
TROUBLE ON THE SELECTION	- 110 -
THE PROFESSIONAL WANDERER	- 111 -
A LITTLE MISTAKE	- 112 -
A STUDY IN THE "NOOD"	- 114 -
A WORD TO TEXAS JACK	- 116 -
THE GROG-AN'-GRUMBLE STEEPLECHASE	- 118 -
BUT WHAT'S THE USE	- 120 -

PREFACE

My acknowledgments of the courtesy of the editors and proprietors of the newspapers in which most of these verses were first published are due and are gratefully discharged on the eve of my departure for England. Chief among them is the Sydney *Bulletin*; others are the Sydney *Town and Country Journal*, *Freeman's Journal*, and *Truth*, and the *New Zealand Mail*.

A few new pieces are included in the collection.

H. L.

Sydney, March 17th, 1900.

"Once I wrote a little poem which I thought was very fine,
And I showed the printer's copy to a critic friend of mine,
First he praised the thing a little...."

THE PORTS OF THE OPEN SEA

DOWN here where the ships loom large in
The gloom when the sea-storms veer,
Down here on the south-west margin
Of the western hemisphere,
Where the might of a world-wide ocean
Round the youngest land rolls free—
Storm-bound from the world's commotion,
Lie the Ports of the Open Sea.

By the bluff where the grey sand reaches
To the kerb of the spray-swept street,
By the sweep of the black sand beaches
From the main-road travellers' feet,
By the heights like a work Titanic,
Begun ere the gods' work ceased,
By a bluff-lined coast volcanic
Lie the Ports of the wild South-east.

By the steeps of the snow-capped ranges,
By the scarped and terraced hills—
Far away from the swift life-changes,
From the wear of the strife that kills—
Where the land in the Spring seems younger
Than a land of the Earth might be—
Oh! the hearts of the rovers hunger
For the Ports of the Open Sea.

But the captains watch and hearken
For a sign of the South Sea wrath—
Let the face of the South-east darken,
And they turn to the ocean path.
Ay, the sea-boats dare not linger,
Whatever the cargo be;
When the South-east lifts a finger
By the Ports of the Open Sea.

South by the bleak Bluff faring,
North where the Three Kings wait,
South-east the tempest daring—
Flight through the storm-tossed strait;
Yonder a white-winged roamer

Struck where the rollers roar—
Where the great green froth-flaked comber
Breaks down on a black-ribbed shore.

For the South-east lands are dread lands
To the sailor in the shrouds,
Where the low clouds loom like headlands,
And the black bluffs blur like clouds.
When the breakers rage to windward
And the lights are masked a-lee,
And the sunken rocks run inward
To a Port of the Open Sea.

But oh! for the South-east weather—
The sweep of the three-days' gale—
When, far through the flax and heather,
The spindrift drives like hail.
Glory to man's creations
That drive where the gale grows gruff,
When the homes of the sea-coast stations
Flash white from the dark'ning bluff!

When the swell of the South-east rouses
The wrath of the Maori sprite,
And the brown folk flee their houses
And crouch in the flax by night,
And wait as they long have waited—
In fear as the brown folk be—
The wave of destruction fated
For the Ports of the Open Sea.
. . . .
Grey cloud to the mountain bases,
Wild boughs that rush and sweep;
On the rounded hills the tussocks
Like flocks of flying sheep;
A lonely storm-bird soaring
O'er tussock, fern and tree;
And the boulder beaches roaring
The Hymn of the Open Sea.

THE THREE KINGS[A]

[A] Three sea-girt pinnacles off North Cape, New Zealand.

THE East is dead and the West is done, and again our course lies thus:—
South-east by Fate and the Rising Sun where the Three Kings wait for us.
When our hearts are young and the world is wide, and the heights seem grand to climb—
We are off and away to the Sydney-side; but the Three Kings bide their time.

'I've been to the West,' the digger said: he was bearded, bronzed and old;
'Ah, the smothering curse of the East is wool, and the curse of the West is gold.
'I went to the West in the golden boom, with Hope and a life-long mate,
'They sleep in the sand by the Boulder Soak, and long may the Three Kings wait.'

'I've had my fling on the Sydney-side,' said a black-sheep to the sea,
'Let the young fool learn when he can't be taught: I've learnt what's good for me.'
And he gazed ahead on the sea-line dim—grown dim in his softened eyes—
With a pain in his heart that was good for him—as he saw the Three Kings rise.

A pale girl sits on the foc'sle head—she is back, Three Kings! so soon;
But it seems to her like a life-time dead since she fled with him 'saloon.'
There is refuge still in the old folks' arms for the child that loved too well;
They will hide her shame on the Southern farm—and the Three Kings will not tell.

'Twas a restless heart on the tide of life, and a false star in the skies
That led me on to the deadly strife where the Southern London lies;
But I dream in peace of a home for me, by a glorious southern sound,
As the sunset fades from a moonlit sea, and the Three Kings show us round.

Our hearts are young and the old hearts old, and life on the farms is slow,
And away in the world there is fame and gold—and the Three Kings watch us go.
Our heads seem wise and the world seems wide, and its heights are ours to climb,
So it's off and away in our youthful pride—but the Three Kings bide our time.

THE OUTSIDE TRACK

THERE were ten of us there on the moonlit quay,
And one on the for'ard hatch;
No straighter mate to his mates than he
Had ever said: 'Len's a match!'
'Twill be long, old man, ere our glasses clink,
'Twill be long ere we grip your hand!—
And we dragged him ashore for a final drink
Till the whole wide world seemed grand.

For they marry and go as the world rolls back,
They marry and vanish and die;
But their spirit shall live on the Outside Track
As long as the years go by.

The port-lights glowed in the morning mist
That rolled from the waters green;
And over the railing we grasped his fist
As the dark tide came between.

We cheered the captain and cheered the crew,
And our mate, times out of mind;
We cheered the land he was going to
And the land he had left behind.

We roared Lang Syne as a last farewell,
But my heart seemed out of joint;
I well remember the hush that fell
When the steamer had passed the point
We drifted home through the public bars,
We were ten times less by one
Who sailed out under the morning stars,
And under the rising sun.

And one by one, and two by two,
They have sailed from the wharf since then;
I have said good-bye to the last I knew,
The last of the careless men.
And I can't but think that the times we had
Were the best times after all,
As I turn aside with a lonely glass
And drink to the bar-room wall.

But I'll try my luck for a cheque Out Back,
Then a last good-bye to the bush;
For my heart's away on the Outside Track,
On the track of the steerage push.

SYDNEY-SIDE

WHERE'S the steward?—Bar-room steward? Berth? Oh, any berth will do—
I have left a three-pound billet just to come along with you.
Brighter shines the Star of Rovers on a world that's growing wide,
But I think I'd give a kingdom for a glimpse of Sydney-Side.

Run of rocky shelves at sunrise, with their base on ocean's bed;
Homes of Coogee, homes of Bondi, and the lighthouse on South Head;
For in loneliness and hardship—and with just a touch of pride—
Has my heart been taught to whisper, 'You belong to Sydney-Side.'

Oh, there never dawned a morning, in the long and lonely days,
But I thought I saw the ferries streaming out across the bays—
And as fresh and fair in fancy did the picture rise again
As the sunrise flushed the city from Woollahra to Balmain.

And the sunny water frothing round the liners black and red,
And the coastal schooners working by the loom of Bradley's Head;
And the whistles and the sirens that re-echo far and wide—
All the life and light and beauty that belong to Sydney-Side.

And the dreary cloud-line never veiled the end of one day more,
But the city set in jewels rose before me from 'The Shore.'
Round the sea-world shine the beacons of a thousand ports o' call,
But the harbour-lights of Sydney are the grandest of them all!

Toiling out beyond Coolgardie—heart and back and spirit broke,
Where the Rover's Star gleams redly in the desert by the 'soak'—
But says one mate to the other, 'Brace your lip and do not fret,
We will laugh on trains and 'buses—Sydney's in the same place yet.'

Working in the South in winter, to the waist in dripping fern,
Where the local spirit hungers for each 'saxpence' that we earn—
We can stand it for a season, for our world is growing wide,
And they all are friends and strangers who belong to Sydney-Side.

'T'other-siders! T'other-siders!' Yet we wake the dusty dead;
It is we that send the backward province fifty years ahead;
We it is that 'trim' Australia—making narrow country wide—
Yet we're always T'other-siders till we sail for Sydney-side.

THE ROVERS

SOME born of homely parents
For ages settled down—
The steady generations
Of village, farm, and town:
And some of dusky fathers
Who wandered since the flood—
The fairest skin or darkest
Might hold the roving blood—

Some born of brutish peasants,
And some of dainty peers,
In poverty or plenty
They pass their early years;
But, born in pride of purple,
Or straw and squalid sin,
In all the far world corners
The wanderers are kin.

A rover or a rebel,
Conceived and born to roam,
As babies they will toddle
With faces turned from home;
They've fought beyond the vanguard
Wherever storm has raged,
And home is but a prison
They pace like lions caged.

They smile and are not happy;
They sing and are not gay;
They weary, yet they wander;
They love, and cannot stay;
They marry, and are single
Who watch the roving star,
For, by the family fireside,
Oh, lonely men *they* are!

They die of peace and quiet—
The deadly ease of life;
They die of home and comfort;
They *live* in storm and strife;
No poverty can tie them,

Nor wealth nor place restrain—
Girl, wife, or child might draw them,
But they'll be gone again!

Across the glowing desert;
Through naked trees and snow;
Across the rolling prairies
The skies have seen them go;
They fought to where the ocean
Receives the setting sun;—
But where shall fight the rovers
When all the lands are won?

They thirst on Greenland snowfields,
On Never-Never sands;
Where man is not to conquer
They conquer barren lands;
They feel that most are cowards,
That all depends on 'nerve,'
They lead who cannot follow,
They rule who cannot serve.

Across the plains and ranges,
Away across the seas,
On blue and green horizons
They camp by twos and threes;
They hold on stormy borders
Of states that trouble earth
The honour of the country
That only gave them birth.

Unlisted, uncommissioned,
Untaught of any school,
In far-away world corners
Unconquered tribes they rule;
The lone hand and revolver—
Sad eyes that never quail—
The lone hand and the rifle
That win where armies fail.

They slumber sound where murder
And treachery are bare—
The pluck of self-reliance,

The pluck of past despair;
Thin brown men in pyjamas—
The thin brown wiry men!—
The helmet and revolver
That lie beside the pen.

Through drought and desolation
They won the way Out Back;
The commonplace and selfish
Have followed on their track;
They conquer lands for others,
For others find the gold,—
But where shall go the rovers
When all the lands are old?

A rover and a rebel—
And so the worlds commence!
Their hearts shall beat as wildly
Ten generations hence;
And when the world is crowded—
'Tis signed and sealed by Fate—
The roving blood will rise to make
The countries desolate.

FOREIGN LANDS

YOU may roam the wide seas over, follow, meet, and cross the sun,
Sail as far as ships can sail, and travel far as trains can run;
You may ride and tramp wherever range or plain or sea expands,
But the crowd has been before you, and you'll not find 'Foreign Lands;'
For the Early Days are over,
And no more the white-winged rover
Sinks the gale-worn coast of England bound for bays in Foreign Lands.

Foreign Lands are in the distance dim and dream-like, faint and far,
Long ago, and over yonder, where our boyhood fancies are,
For the land is by the railway cramped as though with iron bands,
And the steamship and the cable did away with Foreign Lands.
Ah! the days of blue and gold!
When the news was six months old—
But the news was worth the telling in the days of Foreign Lands.

Here we slave the dull years hopeless for the sake of Wool and Wheat—
Here the homes of ugly Commerce—niggard farm and haggard street;
Yet our mothers and our fathers won the life the heart demands—
Less than fifty years gone over, we were born in Foreign Lands.

When the gipsies stole the children still, in village tale and song,
And the world was wide to travel, and the roving spirit strong;
When they dreamed of South Sea Islands, summer seas and coral strands—
Then the bravest hearts of England sailed away to Foreign Lands,
'Fitting foreign'—flood and field—
Half the world and orders sealed—
And the first and best of Europe went to fight in Foreign Lands.

Canvas towers on the ocean—homeward bound and outward bound—
Glint of topsails over islands—splash of anchors in the sound;
Then they landed in the forests, took their strong lives in their hands,
And they fought and toiled and conquered—making homes in Foreign Lands,
Through the cold and through the drought—
Further on and further out—
Winning half the world for England in the wilds of Foreign Lands.

Love and pride of life inspired them when the simple village hearts
Followed Master Will and Harry—gone abroad to 'furrin parts'—

By our townships and our cities, and across the desert sands
Are the graves of those who fought and died for us in Foreign Lands—
Gave their young lives for our sake
(Was it all a grand mistake?)
Sons of Master Will and Harry born abroad in Foreign Lands!

Ah, my girl, our lives are narrow, and in sordid days like these,
I can hate the things that banished 'Foreign Lands across the seas,'
But with all the world before us, God above us—hearts and hands,
I can sail the seas in fancy far away to Foreign Lands.

MARY LEMAINE

JIM DUFF was a 'native,' as wild as could be;
A stealer and duffer of cattle was he,
But back in his youth he had stolen a pearl—
Or a diamond rather—the heart of a girl;
She served with a squatter who lived on the plain,
And the name of the girl it was Mary Lemaine.

'Twas a drear, rainy day and the twilight was done,
When four mounted troopers rode up to the run.
They spoke to the squatter: he asked them all in.
The homestead was small and the walls they were thin;
And in the next room, with a cold in her head,
Our Mary was sewing on buttons—in bed.

She heard a few words, but those words were enough—
The troopers were all on the track of Jim Duff.
The super, his rival, was planning a trap
To capture the scamp in Maginnis's Gap.
'I've warned him before, and I'll do it again;—
I'll save him to-night,' whispered Mary Lemaine.

No petticoat job—there was no time to waste,
The suit she was mending she slipped on in haste,
And five minutes later they gathered in force,
But Mary was off, on the squatter's best horse;
With your hand on your heart, just to deaden the pain,
Ride hard to the ranges, brave Mary Lemaine!

She rode by the ridges all sullen and strange,
And far up long gullies that ran through the range,
Till the rain cleared away, and the tears in her eyes
Caught the beams of the moon from Maginnis's Rise.
A fire in the depths of the gums she espied—
'Who's there?' shouted Jim. 'It is Mary!' she cried.

Next morning the sun rose in splendour again,
And two loving sinners rode out on the plain;
And baffled, and angry, and hungry and damp,
The four mounted troopers rode back to the camp.
But they hushed up the business—the reason is plain,
They all had been 'soft' on fair Mary Lemaine.

The squatter got back all he lost from his mob,
And old Sergeant Kennedy winked at the job;
Jim Duff keeps a shanty far out in the west,
And the sundowners call it the 'Bushranger's Rest.'
But the bushranger lives a respectable life,
And the law never troubles Jim Duff or his wife.

THE SHAKEDOWN ON THE FLOOR

SET me back for twenty summers—
For I'm tired of cities now—
Set my feet in red-soil furrows
And my hands upon the plough,
With the two 'Black Brothers' trudging
On the home stretch through the loam—
While, along the grassy siding,
Come the cattle grazing home.

And I finish ploughing early,
And I hurry home to tea—
There's my black suit on the stretcher,
And a clean white shirt for me;
There's a dance at Rocky Rises,
And, when all the fun is o'er,
For a certain favoured party
There's a shake-down on the floor.

You remember Mary Carey,
Bushmen's favourite at the Rise?
With her sweet small freckled features,
Red-gold hair, and kind grey eyes;
Sister, daughter, to her mother,
Mother, sister, to the rest—
And of all my friends and kindred,
Mary Carey loved me best.

Far too shy, because she loved me,
To be dancing oft with me;
What cared I, because she loved me,
If the world were there to see?
But we lingered by the slip rails
While the rest were riding home,
Ere the hour before the dawning,
Dimmed the great star-clustered dome.

Small brown hands that spread the mattress
While the old folk winked to see
How she'd find an extra pillow
And an extra sheet for me.
For a moment shyly smiling,

She would grant me one kiss more—
Slip away and leave me happy
By the shake-down on the floor.

Rock me hard in steerage cabins,
Rock me soft in wide saloons,
Lay me on the sand-hill lonely
Under waning western moons;
But wherever night may find me
Till I rest for evermore—
I will dream that I am happy
On the shake-down on the floor.

Ah! she often watched at sunset—
For her people told me so—
Where I left her at the slip-rails
More than fifteen years ago.
And she faded like a flower,
And she died, as such girls do,
While, away in Northern Queensland,
Working hard, I never knew.

And we suffer for our sorrows,
And we suffer for our joys,
From the old bush days when mother
Spread the shake-down for the boys.
But to cool the living fever,
Comes a cold breath to my brow,
And I feel that Mary's spirit
Is beside me, even now.

REEDY RIVER

TEN miles down Reedy River
A pool of water lies,
And all the year it mirrors
The changes in the skies,
And in that pool's broad bosom
Is room for all the stars;
Its bed of sand has drifted
O'er countless rocky bars.

Around the lower edges
There waves a bed of reeds,
Where water rats are hidden
And where the wild duck breeds;
And grassy slopes rise gently
To ridges long and low,
Where groves of wattle flourish
And native bluebells grow.

Beneath the granite ridges
The eye may just discern
Where Rocky Creek emerges
From deep green banks of fern;
And standing tall between them,
The grassy sheoaks cool
The hard, blue-tinted waters
Before they reach the pool.

Ten miles down Reedy River
One Sunday afternoon,
I rode with Mary Campbell
To that broad bright lagoon;
We left our horses grazing
Till shadows climbed the peak,
And strolled beneath the sheoaks
On the banks of Rocky Creek.

Then home along the river
That night we rode a race,
And the moonlight lent a glory
To Mary Campbell's face;
And I pleaded for my future

All thro' that moonlight ride,
Until our weary horses
Drew closer side by side.

Ten miles from Ryan's crossing
And five below the peak,
I built a little homestead
On the banks of Rocky Creek;
I cleared the land and fenced it
And ploughed the rich red loam,
And my first crop was golden
When I brought Mary home.
. . . .
Now still down Reedy River
The grassy sheoaks sigh,
And the waterholes still mirror
The pictures in the sky;
And over all for ever
Go sun and moon and stars,
While the golden sand is drifting
Across the rocky bars;

But of the hut I builded
There are no traces now.
And many rains have levelled
The furrows of the plough;
And my bright days are olden,
For the twisted branches wave
And the wattle blossoms golden
On the hill by Mary's grave.

OLD STONE CHIMNEY

THE rising moon on the peaks was blending
Her silver light with the sunset glow,
When a swagman came as the day was ending
Along a path that he seemed to know.
But all the fences were gone or going—
The hand of ruin was everywhere;
The creek unchecked in its course was flowing,
For none of the old clay dam was there.

Here Time had been with his swiftest changes,
And husbandry had westward flown;
The cattle tracks in the rugged ranges
Were long ago with the scrub o'ergrown.
It must have needed long years to soften
The road, that as hard as rock had been;
The mountain path he had trod so often
Lay hidden now with a carpet green.

He thought at times from the mountain courses
He heard the sound of a bullock bell,
The distant gallop of stockmen's horses,
The stockwhip's crack that he knew so well:
But these were sounds of his memory only,
And they were gone from the flat and hill,
For when he listened the place was lonely,
The range was dumb and the bush was still.

The swagman paused by the gap and faltered,
For down the gully he feared to go,
The scene in memory never altered—
The scene before him had altered so.
But hope is strong, and his heart grew bolder,
And over his sorrows he raised his head,
He turned his swag to the other shoulder,
And plodded on with a firmer tread.

Ah, hope is always the keenest hearer,
And fancies much when assailed by fear;
The swagman thought, as the farm drew nearer,
He heard the sounds that he used to hear.
His weary heart for a moment bounded,

For a moment brief he forgot his dread;
For plainly still in his memory sounded
The welcome bark of a dog long dead.

A few steps more and his face grew ghostly,
Then white as death in the twilight grey;
Deserted wholly, and ruined mostly,
The Old Selection before him lay.
Like startled spectres that paused and listened,
The few white posts of the stockyard stood;
And seemed to move as the moonlight glistened
And paled again on the whitened wood.

And thus he came, from a life long banished
To other lands, and of peace bereft,
To find the farm and the homestead vanished,
And only the old stone chimney left.
The field his father had cleared and gardened
Was overgrown with saplings now;
The rain had set and the drought had hardened
The furrows made by a vanished plough.

And this, and this was the longed-for haven
Where he might rest from a life of woe;
He read a name on the mantel graven—
The name was his ere he stained it so.
'And so remorse on my care encroaches—
I have not suffered enough,' he said;
'That name is pregnant with deep reproaches—
The past won't bury dishonoured dead!'

Ah, now he knew it was long years after,
And felt how swiftly a long year speeds;
The hardwood post and the beam and rafter
Had rotted long in the tangled weeds.
He found that time had for years been sowing
The coarse wild scrub on the homestead path,
And saw young trees by the chimney growing,
And mountain ferns on the wide stone hearth.

He wildly thought of the evil courses
That brought disgrace on his father's name;
The escort robbed, and the stolen horses,

The felon's dock with its lasting shame.
'Ah, God! Ah, God! is there then no pardon?'
He cried in a voice that was strained and hoarse;
He fell on the weeds that were once a garden,
And sobbed aloud in his great remorse.

But grief must end, and his heart ceased aching
When pitying sleep to his eye-lids crept,
And home and friends who were lost in waking,
They all came back while the stockman slept.
And when he woke on the empty morrow,
The pain at his heart was a deadened pain;
And bravely bearing his load of sorrow,
He wandered back to the world again.

SONG OF THE OLD BULLOCK-DRIVER

FAR back in the days when the blacks used to ramble
In long single file 'neath the evergreen tree,
The wool-teams in season came down from Coonamble,
And journeyed for weeks on their way to the sea.
'Twas then that our hearts and our sinews were stronger,
For those were the days when the bushman was bred.
We journeyed on roads that were rougher and longer
Than roads where the feet of our grandchildren tread.

With mates who have gone to the great Never-Never,
And mates whom I've not seen for many a day,
I camped on the banks of the Cudgegong River
And yarned at the fire by the old bullock-dray.
I would summon them back from the far Riverina,
From days that shall be from all others distinct,
And sing to the sound of an old concertina
Their rugged old songs where strange fancies were linked.

We never were lonely, for, camping together,
We yarned and we smoked the long evenings away,
And little I cared for the signs of the weather
When snug in my hammock slung under the dray.
We rose with the dawn, were it ever so chilly,
When yokes and tarpaulins were covered with frost,
And toasted the bacon and boiled the black billy,
Where high on the camp-fire the branches were tossed.

On flats where the air was suggestive of 'possums,
And homesteads and fences were hinting of change,
We saw the faint glimmer of appletree blossoms,
And far in the distance the blue of the range;
And here in the rain, there was small use in flogging
The poor, tortured bullocks that tugged at the load,
When down to the axles the waggons were bogging
And traffic was making a marsh of the road.

'Twas hard on the beasts on the terrible pinches,
Where two teams of bullocks were yoked to a load,
And tugging and slipping, and moving by inches,
Half-way to the summit they clung to the road.
And then, when the last of the pinches was bested,

(You'll surely not say that a glass was a sin?)
The bullocks lay down 'neath the gum trees and rested—
The bullockies steered for the bar of the inn.

Then slowly we crawled by the trees that kept tally
Of miles that were passed on the long journey down.
We saw the wild beauty of Capertee Valley,
As slowly we rounded the base of the Crown.
But, ah! the poor bullocks were cruelly goaded
While climbing the hills from the flats and the vales;
'Twas here that the teams were so often unloaded
That all knew the meaning of 'counting your bales.'

And, oh! but the best-paying load that I carried
Was one to the run where my sweetheart was nurse.
We courted awhile, and agreed to get married,
And couple our futures for better or worse.
And as my old feet grew too weary to drag on
The miles of rough metal they met by the way,
My eldest grew up and I gave him the waggon—
He's plodding along by the bullocks to-day.

THE LIGHTS OF COBB AND CO.

FIRE lighted, on the table a meal for sleepy men,
A lantern in the stable, a jingle now and then;
The mail coach looming darkly by light of moon and star,
The growl of sleepy voices—a candle in the bar;
A stumble in the passage of folk with wits abroad;
A swear-word from a bedroom—the shout of 'All aboard!'
'Tchk-tchk! Git-up!' 'Hold fast, there!' and down the range we go;
Five hundred miles of scattered camps will watch for Cobb and Co.

Old coaching towns already 'decaying for their sins,'
Uncounted 'Half-Way Houses,' and scores of 'Ten Mile Inns;'
The riders from the stations by lonely granite peaks;
The black-boy for the shepherds on sheep and cattle creeks;
The roaring camps of Gulgong, and many a 'Digger's Rest;'
The diggers on the Lachlan; the huts of Furthest West;
Some twenty thousand exiles who sailed for weal or woe;
The bravest hearts of twenty lands will wait for Cobb and Co.

The morning star has vanished, the frost and fog are gone,
In one of those grand mornings which but on mountains dawn;
A flask of friendly whisky—each other's hopes we share—
And throw our top-coats open to drink the mountain air.
The roads are rare to travel, and life seems all complete;
The grind of wheels on gravel, the trot of horses' feet,
The trot, trot, trot and canter, as down the spur we go—
The green sweeps to horizons blue that call for Cobb and Co.

We take a bright girl actress through western dust and damps,
To bear the home-world message, and sing for sinful camps,
To wake the hearts and break them, wild hearts that hope and ache—
(Ah! when she thinks of those days her own must nearly break!)
Five miles this side the gold-field, a loud, triumphant shout:
Five hundred cheering diggers have snatched the horses out:
With 'Auld Lang Syne' in chorus through roaring camps they go—
That cheer for her, and cheer for Home, and cheer for Cobb and Co.

Three lamps above the ridges and gorges dark and deep,
A flash on sandstone cuttings where sheer the sidings sweep,
A flash on shrouded waggons, on water ghastly white;
Weird bush and scattered remnants of 'rushes in the night;'
Across the swollen river a flash beyond the ford:

Ride hard to warn the driver! He's drunk or mad, good Lord!'
But on the bank to westward a broad, triumphant glow—
A hundred miles shall see to-night the lights of Cobb and Co.!

Swift scramble up the siding where teams climb inch by inch;
Pause, bird-like, on the summit—then breakneck down the pinch
Past haunted half-way houses—where convicts made the bricks—
Scrub-yards and new bark shanties, we dash with five and six—
By clear, ridge-country rivers, and gaps where tracks run high,
Where waits the lonely horseman, cut clear against the sky;
Through stringy-bark and blue-gum, and box and pine we go;
New camps are stretching 'cross the plains the routes of Cobb and Co.
. . . .
Throw down the reins, old driver—there's no one left to shout;
The ruined inn's survivor must take the horses out.
A poor old coach hereafter!—we're lost to all such things—
No bursts of songs or laughter shall shake your leathern springs
When creeping in unnoticed by railway sidings drear,
Or left in yards for lumber, decaying with the year—
Oh, who'll think how in those days when distant fields were broad
You raced across the Lachlan side with twenty-five on board.

Not all the ships that sail away since Roaring Days are done—
Not all the boats that steam from port, nor all the trains that run,
Shall take such hopes and loyal hearts—for men shall never know
Such days as when the Royal Mail was run by Cobb and Co.
The 'greyhounds' race across the sea, the 'special' cleaves the haze,
But these seem dull and slow to me compared with Roaring Days!
The eyes that watched are dim with age, and souls are weak and slow,
The hearts are dust or hardened now that broke for Cobb and Co.

HOW THE LAND WAS WON

THE future was dark and the past was dead
As they gazed on the sea once more—
But a nation was born when the immigrants said
'Good-bye!' as they stepped ashore!
In their loneliness they were parted thus
Because of the work to do,
A wild wide land to be won for us
By hearts and hands so few.

The darkest land 'neath a blue sky's dome,
And the widest waste on earth;
The strangest scenes and the least like home
In the lands of our fathers' birth;
The loneliest land in the wide world then,
And away on the furthest seas,
A land most barren of life for men—
And they won it by twos and threes!

With God, or a dog, to watch, they slept
By the camp-fires' ghastly glow,
Where the scrubs were dark as the blacks that crept
With 'nulla' and spear held low;
Death was hidden amongst the trees,
And bare on the glaring sand
They fought and perished by twos and threes—
And that's how they won the land!

It was two that failed by the dry creek bed,
While one reeled on alone—
The dust of Australia's greatest dead
With the dust of the desert blown!
Gaunt cheek-bones cracking the parchment skin
That scorched in the blazing sun,
Black lips that broke in a ghastly grin—
And that's how the land was won!

Starvation and toil on the tracks they went,
And death by the lonely way;
The childbirth under the tilt or tent,
The childbirth under the dray!
The childbirth out in the desolate hut

With a half-wild gin for nurse—
That's how the first were born to bear
The brunt of the first man's curse!

They toiled and they fought through the shame of it—
Through wilderness, flood, and drought;
They worked, in the struggles of early days,
Their sons' salvation out.
The white girl-wife in the hut alone,
The men on the boundless run,
The miseries suffered, unvoiced, unknown—
And that's how the land was won.

No armchair rest for the old folk then—
But, ruined by blight and drought,
They blazed the tracks to the camps again
In the big scrubs further out.
The worn haft, wet with a father's sweat,
Gripped hard by the eldest son,
The boy's back formed to the hump of toil—
And that's how the land was won!

And beyond Up Country, beyond Out Back,
And the rainless belt, they ride,
The currency lad and the ne'er-do-weel
And the black sheep, side by side;
In wheeling horizons of endless haze
That disk through the Great North-west,
They ride for ever by twos and by threes—
And that's how they win the rest.

THE BOSS OVER THE BOARD

When he's over a rough and unpopular shed,
With the sins of the bank and the men on his head;
When he musn't look black or indulge in a grin,
And thirty or forty men hate him like Sin—
I am moved to admit—when the total is scored—
That it's just a bit off for the Boss-of-the-board.
I have battled a lot,
But my dream's never soared
To the lonely position of Boss-of-the-board.

'Twas a black-listed shed down the Darling: the Boss
Was a small man to see—though a big man to cross—
We had nought to complain of—except what we thought,
And the Boss didn't boss any more than he ought;
But the Union was booming, and Brotherhood soared,
So we hated like poison the Boss-of-the-board.
We could tolerate 'hands'—
We respected the cook;
But the name of a Boss was a blot in our book.

He'd a row with Big Duggan—a rough sort of Jim—
Or, rather, Jim Duggan was 'laying for' him!
His hate of Injustice and Greed was so deep
That his shearing grew rough—and he ill-used the sheep.
And I fancied that Duggan his manliness lower'd
When he took off his shirt to the Boss-of-the-board,
For the Boss was ten stone,
And the shearer full-grown,
And he might have, they said, let the crawler alone.

Though some of us there wished the fight to the strong,
Yet we knew in our hearts that the shearer was wrong.
And the crawler was plucky, it can't be denied,
For he had to fight Freedom and Justice beside,
But he came up so gamely, as often as floored,
That a blackleg stood up for the Boss-of-the-board!
And the fight was a sight,
And we pondered that night—
'It's surprising how some of those blacklegs can fight!'

Next day at the office, when sadly the wreck
Of Jim Duggan came up like a lamb for his cheque,
Said the Boss, 'Don't be childish! It's all past and gone;
I am short of good shearers. You'd *better* stay on.'
And we fancied Jim Duggan *our* dignity lower'd
When he stopped to oblige a damned Boss-of-the-board.
We said nothing to Jim,
For a joke might be grim,
And the subject, we saw, was distasteful to him.

The Boss just went on as he'd done from the first,
And he favoured Big Duggan no more than the worst;
And when we'd cut out and the steamer came down—
With the hawkers and spielers—to take us to town,
And we'd all got aboard, 'twas Jim Duggan, good Lord!
Who yelled for three cheers for the Boss-of-the-board.
'Twas a bit off, no doubt—
And with Freedom about—
But a lot is forgot when a shed is cut out.

With Freedom of Contract maintained in his shed,
And the curse of the Children of Light on his head,
He's apt to long sadly for sweetheart or wife,
And his views be inclined to the dark side of life.
The Truth must be spread and the Cause must be shored—
But it's just a bit rough on the Boss-of-the-board.
I am all for the Right,
But perhaps (out of sight)
As a son or a husband or father he's white.

WHEN THE LADIES COME TO THE SHEARING SHED

'THE ladies are coming,' the super says
To the shearers sweltering there,
And 'the ladies' means in the shearing shed:
'Don't cut 'em too bad. Don't swear.'
The ghost of a pause in the shed's rough heart,
And lower is bowed each head;
And nothing is heard, save a whispered word,
And the roar of the shearing-shed.

The tall, shy rouser has lost his wits,
And his limbs are all astray;
He leaves a fleece on the shearing-board,
And his broom in the shearer's way.
There's a curse in store for that jackaroo
As down by the wall he slants—
And the ringer bends with his legs askew
And wishes he'd 'patched them pants.'

They are girls from the city. (Our hearts rebel
As we squint at their dainty feet.)
And they gush and say in a girly way
That 'the dear little lambs' are 'sweet.'
And Bill, the ringer, who'd scorn the use
Of a childish word like 'damn,'
Would give a pound that his tongue were loose
As he tackles a lively lamb.

Swift thoughts of homes in the coastal towns—
Or rivers and waving grass—
And a weight on our hearts that we cannot define
That comes as the ladies pass.
But the rouser ventures a nervous dig
In the ribs of the next to him;
And Barcoo says to his pen-mate: 'Twig
The style of the last un, Jim.'

Jim Moonlight gives her a careless glance—
Then he catches his breath with pain—
His strong hand shakes and the sunlights dance
As he bends to his work again.

But he's well disguised in a bristling beard,
Bronzed skin, and his shearer's dress;
And whatever Jim Moonlight hoped or feared
Were hard for his mates to guess.

Jim Moonlight, wiping his broad, white brow,
Explains, with a doleful smile:
'A stitch in the side,' and 'he's all right now'—
But he leans on the beam awhile,
And gazes out in the blazing noon
On the clearing, brown and bare—
She has come and gone, like a breath of June,
In December's heat and glare.

The bushmen are big rough boys at the best,
With hearts of a larger growth;
But they hide those hearts with a brutal jest,
And the pain with a reckless oath.
Though the Bills and Jims of the bush-bard sing
Of their life loves, lost or dead,
The love of a girl is a sacred thing
Not voiced in a shearing-shed.

THE BALLAD OF THE ROUSEABOUT

A ROUSEABOUT of rouseabouts, from any land—or none—
I bear a nick-name of the bush, and I'm—a woman's son;
I came from where I camp'd last night, and, at the day-dawn glow,
I rub the darkness from my eyes, roll up my swag, and go.

Some take the track for bitter pride, some for no pride at all—
(But—to us all the world is wide when driven to the wall)
Some take the track for gain in life, some take the track for loss—
And some of us take up the swag as Christ took up the Cross.

Some take the track for faith in men—some take the track for doubt—
Some flee a squalid home to work their own salvation out.
Some dared not see a mother's tears nor meet a father's face—
Born of good Christian families some leap, head-long, from Grace.

Oh we are men who fought and rose, or fell from many grades;
Some born to lie, and some to pray, we're men of many trades;
We're men whose fathers were and are of high and low degree—
The sea was open to us and we sailed across the sea.

And—were our quarrels wrong or just?—has no place in my song—
We seared our souls in puzzling as to what was right or wrong;
We judge not and we are not judged—'tis our philosophy—
There's something wrong with every ship that sails upon the sea.

From shearing shed to shearing shed we tramp to make a cheque—
Jack Cornstalk and the ne'er-do-weel—the tar-boy and the wreck.
We learn the worth of man to man—and this we learn too well—
The shanty and the shearing shed are warmer spots in hell!

I've humped my swag to Bawley Plain, and further out and on;
I've boiled my billy by the Gulf, and boiled it by the Swan—
I've thirsted in dry lignum swamps, and thirsted on the sand,
And eked the fire with camel dung in Never-Never Land.

I know the track from Spencer's Gulf and north of Cooper's Creek—
Where falls the half-caste to the strong, 'black velvet' to the weak—
(From gold-top Flossie in the Strand to half-caste and the gin—
If they had brains, poor animals! we'd teach them how to sin.)

I've tramped, and camped, and 'shore' and drunk with many mates Out Back—
And every one to me is Jack because the first was Jack—
A 'lifer' sneaked from jail at home—the 'straightest' mate I met—
A 'ratty' Russian Nihilist—a British Baronet!

I know the tucker tracks that feed—or leave one in the lurch—
The 'Burgoo' (Presbyterian) track—the 'Murphy' (Roman Church)—
But more the *man*, and not the *track*, so much as it appears,
For 'battling' is a trade to learn, and I've served seven years.

We're haunted by the past at times—and this is very bad,
And so we drink till horrors come, lest, sober, we go mad—
So much is lost Out Back, so much of hell is realised—
A man might skin himself alive and no one be surprised.

A rouseabout of rouseabouts, above—beneath regard,
I know how soft is this old world, and I have learnt how hard—
A rouseabout of rouseabouts—I know what men can feel,
I've seen the tears from hard eyes slip as drops from polished steel.

I learned what college had to teach, and in the school of men
By camp-fires I have learned, or, say, unlearned it all again;
But this I've learned, that truth is strong, and if a man go straight
He'll live to see his enemy struck down by time and fate!

We hold him true who's true to one however false he be
(There's something wrong with every ship that lies beside the quay);
We lend and borrow, laugh and joke, and when the past is drowned,
We sit upon our swags and smoke and watch the world go round.

YEARS AFTER THE WAR IN AUSTRALIA

THE big rough boys from the runs out back were first where the balls flew free,
And yelled in the slang of the Outside Track: 'By God, it's a Christmas spree!'
'It's not too rusty'—and 'Wool away!—stand clear of the blazing shoots!'—
'Sheep O! Sheep O!'—'We'll cut out to-day'—'Look out for the boss's boots!'—
'What price the tally in camp to-night!'—'What price the boys Out Back!'—
'Go it, you tigers, for Right or Might and the pride of the Outside Track!'—
'Needle and thread!'—'I have broke my comb!'—'Now ride, you flour-bags, ride!'—
'Fight for your mates and the folk at home!'—'Here's for the Lachlan side!'
Those men of the West would sneer and scoff at the gates of hell ajar,
And oft the sight of a head cut off was hailed by a yell for 'Tar!'
. . . .
I heard the push in the Red Redoubt, irate at a luckless shot:
'Look out for the blooming shell, look out!'—'Gor' bli' me, but that's red-hot!'—
'It's Bill the Slogger—poor bloke—he's done. A chunk of the shell was his;
I wish the beggar that fired that gun could get within reach of Liz.'
'Those foreign gunners will give us rats, but I wish it was Bill they missed.'
'I'd like to get at their bleeding hats with a rock in my (something) fist.'

'Hold up, Billy; I'll stick to you; they've hit you under the belt;
If we get the waddle I'll swag you through, if the blazing mountains melt;
You remember the night when the traps got me for stoushing a bleeding Chow,
And you went for 'em proper and laid out three, and I won't forget it now.'
And, groaning and swearing, the pug replied: 'I'm done ... they've knocked me out!
I'd fight them all for a pound a-side, from the boss to the rouseabout.
My nut is cracked and my legs is broke, and it gives me worse than hell;
I trained for a scrap with a twelve-stone bloke, and not with a bursting shell.
You needn't mag, for I knowed, old chum, I *knowed*, old pal, you'd stick;
But you can't hold out till the reg'lars come, and you'd best be nowhere quick.
They've got a force and a gun ashore, both of our wings is broke;
They'll storm the ridge in a minute more, and the best you can do is smoke.'

And Jim exclaimed: 'You can smoke, you chaps, but me—Gor' bli' me, no!
The push that ran from the George-street traps won't run from a foreign foe.
I'll stick to the gun while she makes them sick, and I'll stick to what's left of Bill.'
And they hiss through their blackened teeth: 'We'll stick! by the blazing flame, we will!'
And long years after the war was past, they told in the town and bush
How the ridge of death to the bloody last was held by a Sydney push;
How they fought to the end in a sheet of flame, how they fought with their rifle-stocks,
And earned, in a nobler sense, the name of their ancient weapons—'rocks.'
. . . .
In the western camps it was ever our boast, when 'twas bad for the kangaroo:
'If the enemy's forces take the coast, they must take the mountains, too;
They may force their way by the western line or round by a northern track,
But they won't run short of a decent spree with the men who are left out back!'
When we burst the enemy's ironclads and won by a run of luck,
We whooped as loudly as Nelson's lads when a French three-decker struck;
And when the enemy's troops prevailed the truth was never heard—
We lied like heroes who never failed explaining how that occurred.

You bushmen sneer in the old bush way at the newchum jackeroo,
But 'cuffs-'n'-collers' were out that day, and they stuck to their posts like glue;
I never believed that a dude could fight till a Johnny led us then;
We buried his bits in the rear that night for the honour of George-street men.
And Jim the Ringer—he fought, he did. The regiment nicknamed Jim,
'Old Heads a Caser' and 'Heads a Quid,' but it never was 'tails' with him.
The way that he rode was a racing rhyme, and the way that he finished grand;
He backed the enemy every time, and died in a hand-to-hand!
. . . .
I'll never forget when the ringer and I were first in the Bush Brigade,
With Warrego Bill, from the Live-till-you-Die, in the last grand charge we made.
And Billy died—he was full of sand—he said, as I raised his head:
'I'm full of love for my native land, but a lot too full of lead.
Tell 'em,' said Billy, 'and tell old dad, to look after the cattle pup;'
But his eyes grew bright, though his voice was sad, and he said, as I held

him up:
'I have been happy on western farms. And once, when I first went wrong,
Around my neck were the trembling arms of the girl I'd loved so long.
Far out on the southern seas I've sailed, and ridden where brumbies roam,
And oft, when all on the station failed, I've driven the outlaw home.
I've spent a cheque in a day and night, and I've made a cheque as quick;
I struck a nugget when times were tight, and the stores had stopped our tick.
I've led the field on the old bay mare, and I hear the cheering still,
When mother and sister and *she* were there, and the old man yelled for Bill;
But, save for *her*, could I live my while again in the old bush way,
I'd give it all for the last half-mile in the race we rode to-day!'
And he passed away as the stars came out—he died as old heroes die—
I heard the sound of the distant rout, and the Southern Cross was high.

THE OLD JIMMY WOODSER

THE old Jimmy Woodser comes into the bar,
Unwelcomed, unnoticed, unknown,
Too old and too odd to be drunk with, by far;
And he glides to the end where the lunch baskets are
And they say that he tipples alone.

His frock-coat is green and the nap is no more,
And the style of his hat is at rest.
He wears the peaked collar our grandfathers wore,
The black-ribboned tie that was legal of yore,
And the coat buttoned over his breast.

When first he came in, for a moment I thought
That my vision or wits were astray;
For a picture and page out of Dickens he brought,
'Twas an old file dropped in from the Chancery Court
To a wine-vault just over the way.

But I dreamed as he tasted his bitters to-night,
And the lights in the bar-room grew dim,
That the shades of the friends of that other day's light,
And of girls that were bright in our grandfathers' sight,
Lifted shadowy glasses to him.

And I opened the door as the old man passed out,
With his short, shuffling step and bowed head;
And I sighed, for I felt as I turned me about,
An odd sense of respect—born of whisky no doubt—
For the life that was fifty years dead.

And I thought—there are times when our memory trends
Through the future, as 'twere, on its own—
That I, out of date ere my pilgrimage ends,
In a new fashioned bar to dead loves and dead friends
Might drink like the old man alone:
While they whisper, 'He boozes alone.'

THE CHRIST OF THE 'NEVER'

WITH eyes that seem shrunken to pierce
To the awful horizons of land,
Through the haze of hot days, and the fierce
White heat-waves that flow on the sand;
Through the Never Land westward and nor'ward,
Bronzed, bearded and gaunt on the track,
Quiet-voiced and hard-knuckled, rides forward
The Christ of the Outer Out-back.

For the cause that will ne'er be relinquished
Spite of all the great cynics on earth—
In the ranks of the bush undistinguished
By manner or dress—if by birth—
God's preacher, of churches unheeded—
God's vineyard, though barren the sod—
Plain spokesman where spokesman is needed—
Rough link 'twixt the bushman and God.

He works where the hearts of all nations
Are withered in flame from the sky,
Where the sinners work out their salvations
In a hell-upon-earth ere they die.
In the camp or the lonely hut lying
In a waste that seems out of God's sight,
He's the doctor—the mate of the dying
Through the smothering heat of the night.

By his work in the hells of the shearers,
Where the drinking is ghastly and grim,
Where the roughest and worst of his hearers
Have listened bareheaded to him.
By his paths through the parched desolation
Hot rides and the terrible tramps;
By the hunger, the thirst, the privation
Of his work in the furthermost camps;

By his worth in the light that shall search men
And prove—ay! and justify each—
I place him in front of all churchmen
Who feel not, who *know* not—but preach!

THE CATTLE-DOG'S DEATH

THE plains lay bare on the homeward route,
And the march was heavy on man and brute;
For the Spirit of Drouth was on all the land,
And the white heat danced on the glowing sand.

The best of our cattle-dogs lagged at last,
His strength gave out ere the plains were passed,
And our hearts grew sad when he crept and laid
His languid limbs in the nearest shade.

He saved our lives in the years gone by,
When no one dreamed of the danger nigh,
And the treacherous blacks in the darkness crept
On the silent camp where the drovers slept.

'The dog is dying,' a stockman said,
As he knelt and lifted the shaggy head;
' 'Tis a long day's march ere the run be near,
And he's dying fast; shall we leave him here?'

But the super cried, 'There's an answer there!'
As he raised a tuft of the dog's grey hair;
And, strangely vivid, each man descried
The old spear-mark on the shaggy hide.

We laid a 'bluey' and coat across
The camping pack of the lightest horse,
And raised the dog to his deathbed high,
And brought him far 'neath the burning sky.

At the kindly touch of the stockmen rude
His eyes grew human with gratitude;
And though we parched in the heat that fags,
We gave him the last of the water-bags.

The super's daughter we knew would chide
If we left the dog in the desert wide;
So we brought him far o'er the burning sand
For a parting stroke of her small white hand.

But long ere the station was seen ahead,
His pain was o'er, for the dog was dead;
And the folks all knew by our looks of gloom
'Twas a comrade's corpse that we carried home.

THE SONG OF THE DARLING RIVER

The only national work of the blacks was a dam or dyke of stones across the Darling River at Brewarrina. The stones they carried from Lord knows where—and the Lord knows how. The people of Bourke kept up navigation for months above the town by a dam of sand-bags. The Darling rises in blazing droughts from the Queensland rains. There are banks and beds of good clay and rock along the river.

THE skies are brass and the plains are bare,
Death and ruin are everywhere—
And all that is left of the last year's flood
Is a sickly stream on the grey-black mud;
The salt-springs bubble and quagmires quiver,
And—this is the dirge of the Darling River:

'I rise in the drought from the Queensland rain,
I fill my branches again and again;
I hold my billabongs back in vain,
For my life and my peoples the South Seas drain;
And the land grows old and the people never
Will see the worth of the Darling River.

'I drown dry gullies and lave bare hills,
I turn drought-ruts into rippling rills—
I form fair island and glades all green
Till every bend is a sylvan scene.
I have watered the barren land ten leagues wide!
But in vain I have tried, ah! in vain I have tried
To show the sign of the Great All Giver,
The Word to a people: O! lock your river.

'I want no blistering barge aground,
But racing steamers the seasons round;
I want fair homes on my lonely ways,
A people's love and a people's praise—
And rosy children to dive and swim—
And fair girls' feet in my rippling brim;
And cool, green forests and gardens ever'—
Oh, this is the hymn of the Darling River.

The sky is brass and the scrub-lands glare,
Death and ruin are everywhere;

Thrown high to bleach, or deep in the mud
The bones lie buried by last year's flood.
And the Demons dance from the Never Never
To laugh at the rise of the Darling River.

RAIN IN THE MOUNTAINS

THE valley's full of misty cloud,
Its tinted beauty drowning,
The Eucalypti roar aloud,
The mountain fronts are frowning.

The mist is hanging like a pall
From many granite ledges,
And many a little waterfall
Starts o'er the valley's edges.

The sky is of a leaden grey,
Save where the north is surly,
The driven daylight speeds away,
And night comes o'er us early.

But, love, the rain will pass full soon,
Far sooner than my sorrow,
And in a golden afternoon
The sun may set to-morrow.

A MAY NIGHT ON THE MOUNTAINS

'Tis a wonderful time when these hours begin,
These long 'small hours' of night,
When grass is crisp, and the air is thin,
And the stars come close and bright.
The moon hangs caught in a silvery veil,
From clouds of a steely grey,
And the hard, cold blue of the sky grows pale
In the wonderful Milky Way.

There is something wrong with this star of ours,
A mortal plank unsound,
That cannot be charged to the mighty powers
Who guide the stars around.
Though man is higher than bird or beast,
Though wisdom is still his boast,
He surely resembles Nature least,
And the things that vex her most.

Oh, say, some muse of a larger star,
Some muse of the Universe,
If they who people those planets far
Are better than we, or worse?
Are they exempted from deaths and births,
And have they greater powers,
And greater heavens, and greater earths,
And greater Gods than ours?

Are our lies theirs, and our truth their truth,
Are they cursed for pleasure's sake,
Do they make their hells in their reckless youth
Ere they know what hells they make?
And do they toil through each weary hour
Till the tedious day is o'er,
For food that gives but the fleeting power
To toil and strive for more?

THE NEW CHUM JACKAROO

LET bushmen think as bushmen will,
And say whate'er they choose,
I hate to hear the stupid sneer
At New Chum Jackaroos.

He may not ride as you can ride,
Or do what you can do;
But sometimes you'd seem small beside
The New Chum Jackaroo.

His share of work he never shirks,
And through the blazing drought,
He lives the old things down, and works
His own salvation out.

When older, wiser chums despond
He battles brave of heart—
'Twas he who sailed of old beyond
The margin of the chart.

'Twas he who proved the world was round—
In crazy square canoes;
The lands you're living in were found
By New Chum Jackaroos.

He crossed the deserts hot and bare,
From barren, hungry shores—
The plains that you would scarcely dare
With all your tanks and bores.

He fought a way through stubborn hills
Towards the setting sun—
Your fathers all and Burke and Wills
Were New Chums, every one.

When England fought with all the world
In those brave days gone by,
And all its strength against her hurled,
He held her honour high.

By Southern palms and Northern pines—
Where'er was life to lose—
She held her own with thin red lines
Of New Chum Jackaroos.

Through shot and shell and solitudes,
Wherever feet have gone,
The New Chums fought while eye-glass dudes
And Johnnies led them on.

And though he wear a foppish coat,
And these old things forget,
In stormy times I'd give a vote
For Cuffs and Collars yet.

THE DONS OF SPAIN

THE Eagle screams at the beck of trade, so Spain, as the world goes round,
Must wrestle the right to live or die from the sons of the land she found;
For, as in the days when the buccaneer was abroad on the Spanish Main,
The national honour is one thing dear to the hearts of the Dons of Spain.

She has slaughtered thousands with fire and sword, as the Christian world might know;
We murder millions, but, thank the Lord! we only starve 'em slow.
The times have changed since the days of old, but the same old facts remain—
We fight for Freedom, and God, and Gold, and the Spaniards fight for Spain.

We fought with the strength of the moral right, and they, as their ships went down,
They only fought with the grit to fight and their armour to help 'em drown.
It mattered little what chance or hope, for ever their path was plain,
The Church was the Church, and the Pope the Pope—but the Spaniards fought for Spain.

If Providence struck for the honest thief at times in the battle's din—
If ever it struck at the hypocrite—well, that's where the Turks came in;
But this remains ere we leave the wise to argue it through in vain—
There's something great in the wrong that dies as the Spaniards die for Spain.

The foes of Spain may be kin to us who are English heart and soul,
And proud of our national righteousness and proud of the lands we stole;
But we yet might pause while those brave men die and the death-drink pledge again—
For the sake of the past, if you're doomed, say I, may your death be a grand one, Spain!

Then here's to the bravest of Freedom's foes who ever with death have stood—
For the sake of the courage to die on steel as their fathers died on wood;
And here's a cheer for the flag unfurled in a hopeless cause again,
For the sake of the days when the Christian world was saved by the Dons of Spain.

THE BURSTING OF THE BOOM

THE shipping-office clerks are 'short,' the manager is gruff—
'They cannot make reductions,' and 'the fares are low enough.'
They ship us West with cattle, and we go like cattle too;
And fight like dogs three times a day for what we get to chew....
We'll have the pick of empty bunks and lots of stretching room,
And go for next to nothing at the Bursting of the Boom.

So wait till the Boom bursts!—we'll all get a show:
Then when the Boom bursts is our time to go.
We'll meet 'em coming back in shoals, with looks of deepest gloom,
But we're the sort that battle through at the Bursting of the Boom.

The captain's easy-going when Fremantle comes in sight;
He can't say when you'll get ashore—'perhaps to-morrow night;'
Your coins are few, the charges high; you must not linger here—
You'll get your boxes from the hold 'when she's 'longside the pier.' ...
The launch will foul the gangway, and the trembling bulwarks loom
Above a fleet of harbour craft—at the Bursting of the Boom.

So wait till the Boom bursts!—we'll all get a show;
He'll 'take you for a bob, sir,' and where you want to go.
He'll 'take the big portmanteau, sir, if he might so presume'—
You needn't hump your luggage at the Bursting of the Boom.

It's loafers—Customs-loafers—and you pay and pay again;
They hinder you and cheat you from the gangway to the train;
The pubs and restaurants are full—they haven't room for more;
They charge us each three shillings for a shakedown on the floor;
But, 'Show this gentleman upstairs—the first front parlour room.
We'll see about your luggage, sir'—at the Bursting of the Boom.

So wait till the Boom bursts!—we'll all get a show;
And wait till the Boom bursts, and swear mighty low.
'We mostly charge a pound a week. How do you like the room?'
And 'Show this gentleman the bath'—at the Bursting of the Boom.

I go down to the timber-yard (I cannot face the rent)
To get some strips of oregon to frame my hessian tent;
To buy some scraps of lumber for a table or a shelf:
The boss comes up and says I might just look round for myself;

The foreman grunts and turns away as silent as the tomb—
The boss himself will wait on me at the Bursting of the Boom.

So wait till the Boom bursts!—we'll all get a load.
'You had better take those scraps, sir, they're only in the road.'
'Now, where the hell's the carter?' you'll hear the foreman fume;
And, 'Take that timber round at once!' at the Bursting of the Boom.

Each one-a-penny grocer, in his box of board and tin,
Will think it condescending to consent to take you in;
And not content with twice as much as what is just and right,
They charge and cheat you doubly, for the Boom is at its height.
It's 'Take it now or leave it now;' 'your money or your room;'—
But 'Who's attending Mr. Brown?' at the Bursting of the Boom.

So wait till the Boom bursts!—and take what you can get,
'There's not the slightest hurry, and your bill ain't ready yet.'
They'll call and get your orders until the crack o' doom,
And send them round directly, at the Bursting of the Boom.
. . . .
No Country and no Brotherhood—such things are dead and cold;
A camp from all the lands or none, all mad for love of gold;
Where T'othersider number one makes slave of number two,
And the vilest women of the world the vilest ways pursue;
And men go out and slave and bake and die in agony
In western hells that God forgot, where never man should be.
I feel a prophet in my heart that speaks the one word 'Doom!'
And aye you'll hear the Devil laugh at the Bursting of the Boom.

ANTONY VILLA

A Ballad of Ninety-three

OVER there, above the jetty, stands the mansion of the Vardens,
With a tennis ground and terrace, and a flagstaff in the gardens:
They are gentlemen and ladies—they've been 'toffs' for generations,
But old Varden's been unlucky—lost a lot in speculations.

Troubles gathered fast upon him when the mining bubble 'busted,'
Then the bank suspended payment, where his little all he trusted;
And the butcher and the baker sent their bills in when they read it,
Even John, the Chow that served him, has refused to give him 'cledit.'

And the daughters of the Vardens—they are beautiful as Graces—
But the balcony's deserted, and they rarely show their faces;
And the swells of their acquaintance never seem to venture near them,
And the bailiff says they seldom have a cup of tea to cheer them.

They were butterflies—I always was a common caterpillar,
But I'm sorry for the ladies over there in 'Tony Villa,
Shut up there in 'Tony Villa with the bailiff and their trouble;
And the dried-up reservoir, where my tears were seems to bubble.

Mrs. Rooney thinks it nothing when she sends a brat to 'borry'
Just a pinch of tea and sugar till the grocer comes temorry;'
But it's dif'rent with the Vardens—they would starve to death as soon as
Knuckle down. You know, they weren't raised exactly like the Rooneys!
. . . .
There is gossip in the 'boxes' and the drawing-rooms and gardens—
'Have you heard of Varden's failure? Have you heard about the Vardens?'
And no doubt each toney mother on the Point across the water's
Mighty glad about the downfall of the rivals of her daughters.

(Tho' the poets and the writers say that man to man's inhuman,
I'm inclined to think it's nothing to what woman is to woman,
More especially, the ladies, save perhaps a fellow's mother;
And I think that men are better—they are kinder to each other.)
. . . .
There's a youngster by the jetty gathering cinders from the ashes,
He was known as 'Master Varden' ere the great financial crashes.
And his manner shows the dif'rence 'twixt the nurs'ry and gutter—
But I've seen him at the grocer's buying half a pound of butter.

And his mother fights her trouble in the house across the water,
She is just as proud as Varden, though she was a 'cocky's' daughter;
And at times I think I see her with the flick'ring firelight o'er her,
Sitting pale and straight and quiet, gazing vacantly before her.

There's a slight and girlish figure—Varden's youngest daughter, Nettie—
On the terrace after sunset, when the boat is near the jetty;
She is good and pure and pretty, and her rivals don't deny it,
Though they say that Nettie Varden takes in sewing on the quiet.

(How her sister graced the 'circle,' all unconscious of a lover
In the seedy 'god' who watched her from the gallery above her!
Shade of Poverty was on him, and the light of Wealth upon her,
But perhaps he loved her better than the swells attending on her.)
. . . .
There's a white man's heart in Varden, spite of all the blue blood in him,
There are working men who wouldn't stand and hear a word agin' him;
But his name was never printed by the side of his 'donations,'
Save on hearts that have—in this world—very humble circulations.

He was never stiff or hoggish—he was affable and jolly,
And he'd always say 'Good morning' to the deck hand on the 'Polly;'
He would 'barrack' with the newsboys on the Quay across the ferry,
And he'd very often tip 'em coming home a trifle merry.

But his chin is getting higher, and his features daily harden
(He will not 'give up possession'—there's a lot of fight in Varden);
And the way he steps the gangway! oh, you couldn't but admire it!
Just as proud as ever hero walked the plank aboard a pirate!

He will think about the hardships that his girls were never 'useter,'
And it must be mighty heavy on the thoroughbred old rooster;
But he'll never strike his colours, and I tell a lying tale if
Varden's pride don't kill him sooner than the bankers or the bailiff.

You remember when we often had to go without our dinners,
In the days when Pride and Hunger fought a finish out within us;
And how Pride would come up groggy—Hunger whooping loud and louder—
And the swells are proud as we are; they are just as proud—and prouder.

Yes, the toffs have grit, in spite of all our sneering and our scorning—
What's the crowd? What's that? God help us!— Varden shot himself this

morning!...
There'll be gossip in the 'circle,' in the drawing-rooms and gardens;
But I'm sorry for the family; yes—I'm sorry for the Vardens.

SECOND CLASS WAIT HERE

ON suburban railway stations—you may see them as you pass—
There are signboards on the platforms saying, 'Wait here second class;'
And to me the whirr and thunder and the cluck of running gear
Seem to be for ever saying, saying 'Second class wait here'—
'Wait here second class,
Second class wait here.'
Seem to be for ever saying, saying 'Second class wait here.'

And the second class were waiting in the days of serf and prince,
And the second class are waiting—they've been waiting ever since.
There are gardens in the background, and the line is bare and drear,
Yet they wait beneath a signboard, sneering 'Second class wait here.'

I have waited oft in winter, in the mornings dark and damp,
When the asphalt platform glistened underneath the lonely lamp.
Ghastly on the brick-faced cutting 'Sellum's Soap' and 'Blower's Beer;'
Ghastly on enamelled signboards with their 'Second class wait here.'

And the others seemed like burglars, slouched and muffled to the throats,
Standing round apart and silent in their shoddy overcoats,
And the wind among the wires, and the poplars bleak and bare,
Seemed to be for ever snarling, snarling 'Second class wait there.'

Out beyond the further suburb, 'neath a chimney stack alone,
Lay the works of Grinder Brothers, with a platform of their own;
And I waited there and suffered, waited there for many a year,
Slaved beneath a phantom signboard, telling our class to wait here.

Ah! a man must feel revengeful for a boyhood such as mine.
God! I hate the very houses near the workshop by the line;
And the smell of railway stations, and the roar of running gear,
And the scornful-seeming signboards, saying 'Second class wait here.'

There's a train with Death for driver, which is ever going past,
And there are no class compartments, and we all must go at last
To the long white jasper platform with an Eden in the rear;
And there won't be any signboards, saying 'Second class wait here.'

THE SHIPS THAT WON'T GO DOWN

WE hear a great commotion
'Bout the ship that comes to grief,
That founders in mid-ocean,
Or is driven on a reef;
Because it's cheap and brittle
A score of sinners drown.
But we hear but mighty little
Of the ships that won't go down.

Here's honour to the builders—
The builders of the past;
Here's honour to the builders
That builded ships to last;
Here's honour to the captain,
And honour to the crew;
Here's double-column head-lines
To the ships that battle through.

They make a great sensation
About famous men that fail,
That sink a world of chances
In the city morgue or gaol,
Who drink, or blow their brains out,
Because of 'Fortune's frown.'
But we hear far too little
Of the men who won't go down.

The world is full of trouble,
And the world is full of wrong,
But the heart of man is noble,
And the heart of man is strong!
They say the sea sings dirges,
But I would say to you
That the wild wave's song's a pæan
For the men that battle through.

THE MEN WE MIGHT HAVE BEEN

WHEN God's wrath-cloud is o'er me,
Affrighting heart and mind;
When days seem dark before me,
And days seem black behind;
Those friends who think they know me—
Who deem their insight keen—
They ne'er forget to show me
The man I might have been.

He's rich and independent,
Or rising fast to fame;
His bright star is ascendant,
The country knows his name;
His houses and his gardens
Are splendid to be seen;
His fault the wise world pardons—
The man I might have been.

His fame and fortune haunt me;
His virtues wave me back;
His name and prestige daunt me
When I would take the track;
But you, my friend true-hearted—
God keep our friendship green!—
You know how I was parted
From all I might have been.

But what avails the ache of
Remorse or weak regret?
We'll battle for the sake of
The men we might be yet!
We'll strive to keep in sight of
The brave, the true, and clean,
And triumph yet in spite of
The men we might have been.

THE WAY OF THE WORLD

WHEN fairer faces turn from me,
And gayer friends grow cold,
And I have lost through poverty
The friendship bought, with gold;
When I have served the selfish turn
Of some all-worldly few,
And Folly's lamps have ceased to burn,
Then I'll come back to you.

When my admirers find I'm not
The rising star they thought,
And praise or blame is all forgot
My early promise brought;
When brighter rivals lead a host
Where once I led a few,
And kinder times reward their boast,
Then I'll come back to you.

You loved me, not for what I had
Or what I might have been.
You saw the good, but not the bad,
Was kind, for that between.
I know that you'll forgive again—
That you will judge me true;
I'll be too tired to explain
When I come back to you.

THE BATTLING DAYS

SO, sit you down in a straight-backed chair, with your pipe and your wife content,
And cross your knees with your wisest air, and preach of the 'days misspent;'
Grown fat and moral apace, old man! you prate of the change 'since then'—
In spite of all, I'd as lief be back in those hard old days again.

They were hard old days; they were battling days; they were cruel at times—but then,
In spite of all, I would rather be back in those hard old days again.
The land was barren to sow wild oats in the days when we sowed our own—
('Twas little we thought or our friends believed that ours would ever be sown)
But the wild oats wave on their stormy path, and they speak of the hearts of men—
I would sow a crop if I had my time in those hard old days again.

We travel first, or we go saloon—on the planned-out trips we go,
With those who are neither rich nor poor, and we find that the life is slow;
It's 'a pleasant trip' where they cried, 'Good luck!'
There was fun in the steerage then—
In spite of all, I would fain be back in those vagabond days again.

On Saturday night we've a pound to spare—a pound for a trip down town—
We took more joy in those hard old days for a hardly spared half-crown;
We took more pride in the pants we patched than the suits we have had since then—
In spite of all, I would rather be back in those comical days again.

'Twas We and the World—and the rest go hang—as the Outside tracks we trod;
Each thought of himself as a man and mate, and not as a martyred god;
The world goes wrong when your heart is strong—and this is the way with men—
The world goes right when your liver is white, and you preach of the change 'since then.'

They were hard old days; they were battling days; they were cruel times—
but then,
In spite of all, we shall live to-night in those hard old days again.

WRITTEN AFTERWARDS

SO the days of my tramping are over,
And the days of my riding are done—
I'm about as content as a rover
Will ever be under the sun;
I write, after reading your letter—
My pipe with old memories rife—
And I feel in a mood that had better
Not meet the true eyes of the wife.

You must never admit a suggestion
That old things are good to recall;
You must never consider the question:
'Was I happier then, after all?'
You must banish the old hope and sorrow
That make the sad pleasures of life,
You must live for To-day and To-morrow
If you want to be just to the wife.

I have changed since the first day I kissed her.
Which is due—Heaven bless her!—to her;
I'm respected and trusted—I'm 'Mister,'
Addressed by the children as 'Sir.'
And I feel the respect without feigning—
But you'd laugh the great laugh of your life
If you only saw me entertaining
An old lady friend of the wife.

By-the-way, when you're writing, remember
That you never went drinking with me,
And forget our last night of December,
Lest our sev'ral accounts disagree.
And, for my sake, old man, you had better
Avoid the old language of strife,
For the technical terms of your letter
May be misunderstood by the wife.

Never hint of the girls appertaining
To the past (when you're writing again),
For they take such a lot of explaining,
And you know how I hate to explain.
There are some things, we know to our sorrow,

That cut to the heart like a knife,
And your past is To-day and To-morrow
If you want to be true to the wife.

I believe that the creed we were chums in
Was grand, but too abstract and bold,
And the knowledge of life only comes in
When you're married and fathered and old.
And it's well. You may travel as few men,
You may stick to a mistress for life;
But the world, as it is, born of woman
Must be seen through the eyes of the wife.

No doubt you are dreaming as *I* did
And going the careless old pace,
While my future grows dull and decided,
And the world narrows down to the Place.
Let it be. If my 'treason's' resented,
You may do worse, old man, in your life;
Let me dream, too, that I am contented—
For the sake of a true little wife.

THE UNCULTURED RHYMER TO HIS CULTURED CRITICS

FIGHT through ignorance, want, and care—
Through the griefs that crush the spirit;
Push your way to a fortune fair,
And the smiles of the world you'll merit.
Long, as a boy, for the chance to learn—
For the chance that Fate denies you;
Win degrees where the Life-lights burn,
And scores will teach and advise you.

My cultured friends! you have come too late
With your bypath nicely graded;
I've fought thus far on my track of Fate,
And I'll follow the rest unaided.
Must I be stopped by a college gate
On the track of Life encroaching?
Be dumb to Love, and be dumb to Hate,
For the lack of a college coaching?

You grope for Truth in a language dead—
In the dust 'neath tower and steeple!
What know you of the tracks we tread?
And what know you of our people?
'I must read this, and that, and the rest,'
And write as the cult expects me?—
I'll read the book that may please me best,
And write as my heart directs me!

You were quick to pick on a faulty line
That I strove to put my soul in:
Your eyes were keen for a 'dash' of mine
In the place of a semi-colon—
And blind to the rest. And is it for such
As you I must brook restriction?
'I was taught too little?' I learnt too much
To care for a pedant's diction!

Must I turn aside from my destined way
For a task your Joss would find me?
I come with strength of the living day,
And with half the world behind me;

I leave you alone in your cultured halls
To drivel and croak and cavil:
Till your voice goes further than college walls,
Keep out of the tracks we travel!

THE WRITER'S DREAM

A writer wrote of the hearts of men, and he followed their tracks afar;
For his was a spirit that forced his pen to write of the things that are.
His heart grew tired of the truths he told, for his life was hard and grim;
His land seemed barren, its people cold—yet the world was dear to him;—
So he sailed away from the Streets of Strife, he travelled by land and sea,
In search of a people who lived a life as life in the world should be.

And he reached a spot where the scene was fair, with forest and field and wood,
And all things came with the seasons there, and each of its kind was good;
There were mountain-rivers and peaks of snow, there were lights of green and gold,
And echoing caves in the cliffs below, where a world-wide ocean rolled.
The lives of men from the wear of Change and the strife of the world were free—
For Steam was barred by the mountain-range and the rocks of the Open Sea.

And the last that were born of a noble race—when the page of the South was fair—
The last of the conquered dwelt in peace with the last of the victors there.
He saw their hearts with the author's eyes who had written their ancient lore,
And he saw their lives as he'd dreamed of such—ah! many a year before.
And 'I'll write a book of these simple folk ere I to the world return,
'And the cold who read shall be kind for these—and the wise who read shall learn.

'Never again in a song of mine shall a jarring note be heard:
'Never again shall a page or line be marred by a bitter word;
'But love and laughter and kindly hours will the book I'll write recall,
'With chastening tears for the loss of one, and sighs for their sorrows all.
'Old eyes will light with a kindly smile, and the young eyes dance with glee—
'And the heart of the cynic will rest awhile for my simple folk and me.'

The lines ran on as he dipped his pen—ran true to his heart and ear—
Like the brighter pages of memory when every line is clear.
The pictures came and the pictures passed, like days of love and light—
He saw his chapters from first to last, and he thought it grand to write.

And the writer kissed his girlish wife, and he kissed her twice for pride:
' 'Tis a book of love, though a book of life! and a book *you'll* read!' he cried.

He was blind at first to each senseless slight (for shabby and poor he came)
From local 'Fashion' and mortgaged pride that scarce could sign its name.
What dreamer would dream of such paltry pride in a scene so fresh and fair?
But the local spirit intensified—with its pitiful shams—was there;
There were cliques wherever two houses stood (no rest for a family ghost!)
They hated each other as women could—but they hated the stranger most.

The writer wrote by day and night and he cried in the face of Fate—
I'll cleave to my dream of life in spite of the cynical ghosts that wait.
' 'Tis the shyness born of their simple lives,' he said to the paltry pride—
(The homely tongues of the simple wives ne'er erred on the generous side)—
'They'll prove me true and they'll prove me kind ere the year of grace be passed,'
But the ignorant whisper of 'axe to grind!' went home to his heart at last.

The writer sat by his drift-wood fire three nights of the South-east gale,
His pen lay idle on pages vain, for his book was a fairy tale.
The world-wise lines of an elder age were plain on his aching brow,
As he sadly thought of each brighter page that would never be written now.
'I'll write no more!' But he bowed his head, for his heart was in Dreamland yet—
'The pages written I'll burn,' he said, 'and the pages thought forget.'

But he heard the hymn of the Open Sea, and the old fierce anger burned,
And he wrenched his heart from its dreamland free as the fire of his youth returned:—
'The weak man's madness, the strong man's scorn—the rebellious hate of youth
From a deeper love of the world are born! And the cynical ghost is Truth!'
And the writer rose with a strength anew wherein Doubt could have no part;
'I'll write my book and it *shall* be true—the truth of a writer's heart.

'Ay! cover the wrong with a fairy tale—who never knew want or care—
A bright green scum on a stagnant pool that will reek the longer there.
You may starve the writer and buy the pen—you may drive it with want and fear—
But the lines run false in the hearts of men—and false to the writer's ear.

The bard's a rebel and strife his part, and he'll burst from his bonds anew,
Till all pens write from a single heart! And so may the dream come true.
. . . .
' 'Tis ever the same in the paths of men where money and dress are all,
The crawler will bully whene'er he can, and the bully who can't will crawl.
And this is the creed in the local hole, where the souls of the selfish rule;
Borrow and cheat while the stranger's green, then sneer at the simple fool.
Spit your spite at the men whom Fate has placed in the head-race first,
And hate till death, with a senseless hate, the man you have injured worst!

'There are generous hearts in the grinding street, but the Hearts of the World go west;
For the men who toil in the dust and heat of the barren lands are best!
'The stranger's hand to the stranger, yet—for a roving folk are mine—
'The stranger's store for the stranger set—and the camp-fire glow the sign!
'The generous hearts of the world, we find, thrive best on the barren sod,
'And the selfish thrive where Nature's kind (they'd bully or crawl to God!)

'I was born to write of the things that are! and the strength was given to me;
'I was born to strike at the things that mar the world as the world should be!
'By the dumb heart-hunger and dreams of youth, by the hungry tracks I've trod—
'I'll fight as a man for the sake of truth, nor pose as a martyred god.
'By the heart of "Bill" and the heart of "Jim," and the men that *their* hearts deem "white,"
'By the handgrips fierce, and the hard eyes dim with forbidden tears!—I'll write!

'I'll write untroubled by cultured fools, or the dense that fume and fret—
'For against the wisdom of all their schools I would stake mine instinct yet!
For the cynical strain in the writer's song is the *world*, not *he*, to blame,
And I'll write as I think, in the knowledge strong that thousands think the same;
And the men who fight in the Dry Country grim battles by day, by night,
Will believe in me, and will stand by me, and will say to the world, "He's right!"'

THE JOLLY DEAD MARCH

If I ever be worthy or famous—
Which I'm sadly beginning to doubt—
When the angel whose place 'tis to name us
Shall say to my spirit, 'Pass out!'
I wish for no sniv'lling about me
(My work was the work of the land),
But I hope that my country will shout me
The price of a decent brass band.

Thump! thump! of the drum and 'Ta-ra-rit,'
Thump! thump! and the music—it's grand,
If only in dreams, or in spirit,
To ride or march after the band!
And myself and my mourners go straying,
And strolling and drifting along
With a band in the front of us playing
The tune of an old battle song!

I ask for no 'turn-out' to bear me;
I ask not for railings or slabs,
And spare me! my country—oh, spare me!
The hearse and the long string of cabs!
I ask not the baton or 'starts' of
The bore with the musical ear,
But the music that's blown from the hearts of
The men who work hard and drink beer.

And let 'em strike up 'Annie Laurie,'
And let them burst out with 'Lang Syne'—
Twin voices of sadness and glory,
That have ever been likings of mine.
And give the French war-hymn deep-throated
The Watch of the Germans between,
And let the last mile be devoted
To 'Britannia' and 'Wearing the Green.'

And if, in the end—more's the pity—
There is fame more than money to spare—
There's a van-man I know in the city
Who'll convey me, right side up with care.
True sons of Australia, and noble,

Have gone from the long dusty way,
While the sole mourner fought down his trouble
With his pipe on the shaft of the dray.
But let them strike up 'Annie Laurie,' &c.

And my spirit will join the procession—
Will pause, if it may, on the brink—
Nor feel the least shade of depression
When the mourners drop out for a drink;
It may be a hot day in December,
Or a cold day in June it may be,
And the drink will but help them remember
The good points the world missed in me.
And help 'em to love 'Annie Laurie,'
And help 'em to raise 'Auld Lang Syne,' &c.

'Unhook the West Port' for an orphan,
An old digger chorus revive—
If you don't hear a whoop from the coffin,
I am *not* being buried alive.
But I'll go with a spirit less bitter
Than mine own on the earth may have been,
And, perhaps, to save trouble, Saint Peter
Will pass me, two comrades between.

And let them strike up 'Annie Laurie,'
And let 'em burst out with 'Lang Syne,'
Twin voices of sadness and glory
That have ever been likings of mine.
Let them swell the French war-hymn deep-throated
(And I'll not buck at 'God Save the Queen'),
But let the last mile be devoted
To 'Britannia' and 'Wearing the Green.'

Thump! thump! of the drums we inherit—
War-drums of my dreams! Oh it's grand,
If only in fancy or spirit,
To ride or march after a band!
And we, the World-Battlers, go straying
And loving and laughing along—
With Hope in the lead of us playing
The tune of a life-battle song!

MY LITERARY FRIEND

Once I wrote a little poem which I thought was very fine,
And I showed the printer's copy to a critic friend of mine,
First he praised the thing a little, then he found a little fault;
'The ideas are good,' he muttered, 'but the rhythm seems to halt.'

So I straighten'd up the rhythm where he marked it with his pen,
And I copied it and showed it to my clever friend again.
'You've improved the metre greatly, but the rhymes are bad,' he said,
As he read it slowly, scratching surplus wisdom from his head.

So I worked as he suggested (I believe in taking time),
And I burnt the 'midnight taper' while I straightened up the rhyme.
'It is better now,' he muttered, 'you go on and you'll succeed,
It has got a ring about it—the ideas are what you need.'

So I worked for hours upon it (I go on when I commence),
And I kept in view the rhythm and the jingle and the sense,
And I copied it and took it to my solemn friend once more—
It reminded him of something he had somewhere read before.
. . . .
Now the people say I'd never put such horrors into print
If I wasn't too conceited to accept a friendly hint,
And my dearest friends are certain that I'd profit in the end
If I'd always show my copy to a literary friend.

MARY CALLED HIM 'MISTER'

THEY'd parted but a year before—she never thought he'd come,
She stammer'd, blushed, held out her hand, and called him *'Mister* Gum.'
How could he know that all the while she longed to murmur 'John.'
He called her 'Miss le Brook,' and asked how she was getting on.

They'd parted but a year before; they'd loved each other well,
But he'd been to the city, and he came back *such* a swell.
They longed to meet in fond embrace, they hungered for a kiss—
But Mary called him 'Mister,' and the idiot called her 'Miss.'

He stood and lean'd against the door—a stupid chap was he—
And, when she asked if he'd come in and have a cup of tea,
He looked to left, he looked to right, and then he glanced behind,
And slowly doffed his cabbage-tree, and said he 'didn't mind.'

She made a shy apology because the meat was tough,
And then she asked if he was sure his tea was sweet enough;
He stirred the tea and sipped it twice, and answer'd 'plenty, quite;'
And cut the smallest piece of beef and said that it was 'right.'

She glanced at him at times and cough'd an awkward little cough;
He stared at anything but her and said, 'I must be off.'
That evening he went riding north—a sad and lonely ride—
She locked herself inside her room, and there sat down and cried.

They'd parted but a year before, they loved each other well—
But she was such a country girl and he was such a swell;
They longed to meet in fond embrace, they hungered for a kiss—
But Mary called him 'Mister' and the idiot called her 'Miss.'

REJECTED

SHE says she's very sorry, as she sees you to the gate;
You calmly say 'Good-bye' to her while standing off a yard,
Then you lift your hat and leave her, walking mighty stiff and straight—
But you're hit, old man—hit hard.

In your brain the words are burning of the answer that she gave,
As you turn the nearest corner and you stagger just a bit;
But you pull yourself together, for a man's strong heart is brave
When it's hit, old man—hard hit.

You might try to drown the sorrow, but the drink has no effect;
You cannot stand the barmaid with her coarse and vulgar wit;
And so you seek the street again, and start for home direct,
When you're hit, old man—hard hit.

You see the face of her you lost, the pity in her smile—
Ah! she is to the barmaid as is snow to chimney grit;
You're a better man and nobler in your sorrow, for a while,
When you're hit, old man—hard hit.

And, arriving at your lodgings, with a face of deepest gloom,
You shun the other boarders and your manly brow you knit;
You take a light and go upstairs directly to your room—
But the whole house knows you're hit.

You clutch the scarf and collar, and you tear them from your throat,
You rip your waistcoat open like a fellow in a fit;
And you fling them in a corner with the made-to-order coat,
When you're hit, old man—hard hit.

You throw yourself, despairing, on your narrow little bed,
Or pace the room till someone starts with 'Skit! cat!—skit!'
And then lie blindly staring at the plaster overhead—
You are hit, old man—hard hit.

It's doubtful whether vanity or love has suffered worst,
So neatly in our nature are those feelings interknit,
Your heart keeps swelling up so bad, you wish that it would burst,
When you're hit, old man—hard hit.

You think and think, and think, and think, till you go mad almost;
Across your sight the spectres of the bygone seem to flit;
The very girl herself seems dead, and comes back as a ghost,
When you're hit, like this—hard hit.

You know that it's all over—you're an older man by years,
In the future not a twinkle, in your black sky not a split.
Ah! you'll think it well that women have the privilege of tears,
When you're hit, old man—hard hit.

You long and hope for nothing but the rest that sleep can bring,
And you find that in the morning things have brightened up a bit;
But you're dull for many evenings, with a cracked heart in a sling,
When you're hit, old man—hard hit.

O'HARA, J.P.

JAMES PATRICK O'HARA, the Justice of Peace,
He bossed the P.M. and he bossed the police;
A parent, a deacon, a landlord was he—
A townsman of weight was O'Hara, J.P.

He gave out the prizes, foundation-stones laid,
He shone when the Governor's visit was paid;
And twice re-elected as Mayor was he—
The flies couldn't roost on O'Hara, J.P.

Now Sandy M'Fly, of the Axe-and-the-Saw,
Was charged with a breach of the licensing law—
He sold after hours whilst talking too free
On matters concerning O'Hara, J.P.

And each contradicted the next witness flat,
Concerning back parlours, side-doors, and all that;
'Twas very conflicting, as all must agree—
Ye'd betther take care!' said O'Hara, J.P.

But 'Baby,' the barmaid, her evidence gave—
A poor, timid darling who tried to be brave—
'Now, *don't* be afraid—if it's frightened ye be—
Speak out, my good girl,' said O'Hara, J.P.

Her hair was so golden, her eyes were so blue,
Her face was so fair and her words seemed so true—
So green in the ways of sweet women was he
That she jolted the heart of O'Hara, J.P.

He turned to the other grave Justice of Peace,
And whispered, 'You can't always trust the police;
'I'll visit the premises during the day,
And see for myself,' said O'Hara, Jay Pay.
(*Case postponed.*)
. . . .
'Twas early next morning, or late the same night—
' 'Twas early next morning' we think would be right—
And sounds that betokened a breach of the law
Escaped through the cracks of the Axe-and-the-Saw.

And Constable Dogherty, out in the street,
Met Constable Clancy a bit off his beat;
He took him with finger and thumb by the ear,
And led him around to a lane in the rear.

He pointed a blind where strange shadows were seen—
Wild pantomime hinting of revels within—
'We'll drop on M'Fly, if you'll listen to me,
And prove we are right to O'Hara, J.P.'

But Clancy was up to the lay of the land,
He cautiously shaded his mouth with his hand—
'Wisht, man! Howld yer whisht! or it's ruined we'll be,
It's the justice himself—it's O'Hara, J.P.'

They hish'd and they whisted, and turned themselves round,
And got themselves off like two cats on wet ground;
Agreeing to be, on their honour as men,
A deaf-dumb-and-blind institution just then.

Inside on a sofa, two barmaids between,
With one on his knee was a gentleman seen;
And any chance eye at the keyhole could see
In less than a wink 'twas O'Hara, J.P.

The first in the chorus of songs that were sung,
The loudest that laughed at the jokes that were sprung,
The guest of the evening, the soul of the spree—
The daddy of all was O'Hara, J.P.

And hard-cases chuckled, and hard-cases said
That Baby and Alice conveyed him to bed—
In subsequent storms it was painful to see
Those hard-cases side with the sinful J.P.

Next day, in the court, when the case came in sight,
O'Hara declared he was satisfied quite;
The case was dismissed—it was destined to be
The final ukase of O'Hara, J.P.

The law and religion came down on him first—
The Christian was hard but his wife was the worst!

Half ruined and half driven crazy was he—
It made an old man of O'Hara, J.P.

Now, young men who come from the bush, do you hear?
Who know not the power of barmaids and beer—
Don't see for yourself! from temptation steer free,
Remember the fall of O'Hara, J.P.

BILL AND JIM FALL OUT

BILL and Jim are mates no longer—they would scorn the name of mate—
Those two bushmen hate each other with a soul-consuming hate;
Yet erstwhile they were as brothers should be (tho' they never will):
Ne'er were mates to one another half so true as Jim and Bill.

Bill was one of those who have to argue every day or die—
Though, of course, he swore 'twas Jim who always itched to argufy.
They would, on most abstract subjects, contradict each other flat
And at times in lurid language—they were mates in spite of that.

Bill believed the Bible story *re* the origin of him—
He was sober, he was steady, he was orthodox; while Jim,
Who, we grieve to state, was always getting into drunken scrapes,
Held that man degenerated from degenerated apes.

Bill was British to the backbone, he was loyal through and through;
Jim declared that Blucher's Prussians won the fight at Waterloo,
And he hoped the coloured races would in time wipe out the white—
And it rather strained their mateship, but it didn't burst it quite.

They battled round in Maoriland—they saw it through and through—
And argued on the rata, what it was and how it grew;
Bill believed the vine grew downward, Jim declared that it grew up—
Yet they always shared their fortunes to the final bite and sup.
Night after night they argued how the kangaroo was born,
And each one held the other's stupid theories in scorn,
Bill believed it was 'born inside,' Jim declared it was born out—
Each as to his own opinions never had the slightest doubt.
They left the earth to argue and they went among the stars,
Re conditions atmospheric, Bill believed 'the hair of Mars
Was too thin for human bein's to exist in mortal states.'
Jim declared it was too thick, if anything—yet they were mates
Bill for Freetrade—Jim, Protection—argued as to which was best
For the welfare of the workers—and their mateship stood the test!
They argued over what they meant and didn't mean at all,
And what they said and didn't—and were mates in spite of all.
Till one night *the two together* tried to light a fire in camp,
When they had a leaky billy and the wood was scarce and damp.
And ... No matter: let the moral be distinctly understood:
One alone should tend the fire, while the other brings the wood.

THE PAROO

IT was a week from Christmas-time,
As near as I remember,
And half a year since in the rear
We'd left the Darling Timber.
The track was hot and more than drear;
The long day seemed forever;
But now we knew that we were near
Our camp—the Paroo River.

With blighted eyes and blistered feet,
With stomachs out of order,
Half mad with flies and dust and heat
We'd crossed the Queensland Border.
I longed to hear a stream go by
And see the circles quiver;
I longed to lay me down and die
That night on Paroo River.

'Tis said the land out West is grand—
I do not care who says it—
It isn't even decent scrub,
Nor yet an honest desert;
It's plagued with flies, and broiling hot,
A curse is on it ever;
I really think that God forgot
The country round that river.

My mate—a native of the land—
In fiery speech and vulgar,
Condemned the flies and cursed the sand,
And doubly damned the mulga.
He peered ahead, he peered about—
A bushman he, and clever—
'Now mind you keep a sharp look-out;
'We must be near the river.'

The 'nose-bags' heavy on each chest
(God bless one kindly squatter!)
With grateful weight our hearts they pressed—
We only wanted water.
The sun was setting (in the west)

In colour like a liver—
We'd fondly hoped to camp and rest
That night on Paroo River.

A cloud was on my mate's broad brow,
And once I heard him mutter:
'I'd like to see the Darling now,
'God bless the Grand Old Gutter!'
And now and then he stopped and said
In tones that made me shiver—
'It cannot well be on ahead,
'I think we've crossed the river.'

But soon we saw a strip of ground
That crossed the track we followed—
No barer than the surface round,
But just a little hollowed.
His brows assumed a thoughtful frown—
This speech he did deliver:
'I wonder if we'd best go down
'Or up the blessed river?'

'But where,' said I, ' 's the blooming stream?'
And he replied, 'We're at it!'
I stood awhile, as in a dream,
'Great Scott!' I cried, 'is *that* it?
'Why, that is some old bridle-track!'
He chuckled, 'Well, I never!
'It's nearly time you came out-back—
'This *is* the Paroo River!'

No place to camp—no spot of damp—
No moisture to be seen there;
If e'er there was it left no sign
That it had ever been there.
But ere the morn, with heart and soul
We'd cause to thank the Giver—
We found a muddy water-hole
Some ten miles down the river.

THE GREEN-HAND ROUSEABOUT

CALL this hot? I beg your pardon. Hot!—you don't know what it means.
(What's that, waiter? lamb or mutton! Thank you—mine is beef and greens.
Bread and butter while I'm waiting. Milk? Oh, yes—a bucketful.)
I'm just in from west the Darling, 'picking-up' and 'rolling wool.'

Mutton stewed or chops for breakfast, dry and tasteless, boiled in fat;
Bread or brownie, tea or coffee—two hours' graft in front of that;
Legs of mutton boiled for dinner—mutton greasy-warm for tea—
Mutton curried (gave my order, beef and plenty greens for me.)

Breakfast, curried rice and mutton till your innards sacrifice,
And you sicken at the colour and the smell of curried rice.
All day long with living mutton—bits and belly-wool and fleece;
Blinded by the yoke of wool, and shirt and trousers stiff with grease,
Till you long for sight of verdure, cabbage-plots and water clear,
And you crave for beef and butter as a boozer craves for beer.
. . . .
Dusty patch in baking mulga—glaring iron hut and shed—
Feel and smell of rain forgotten—water scarce and feed-grass dead.
Hot and suffocating sunrise—all-pervading sheep-yard smell—
Stiff and aching green-hand stretches—'Slushy' rings the bullock-bell—
Pint of tea and hunk of brownie—sinners string towards the shed—
Great, black, greasy crows round carcass—screen behind of dust-cloud red.

Engine whistles. 'Go it, tigers!' and the agony begins,
Picking up for seven devils out of Hades—for my sins;
Picking up for seven devils, seven demons out of Hell!
Sell their souls to get the bell-sheep—half a-dozen Christs they'd sell!
Day grows hot as where they come from—too damned hot for men or brutes;
Roof of corrugated iron, six-foot-six above the shoots!

Whiz and rattle and vibration, like an endless chain of trams;
Blasphemy of five-and-forty—prickly heat—and stink of rams!
'Barcoo' leaves his pen-door open and the sheep come bucking out;
When the rouser goes to pen them, 'Barcoo' blasts the rouseabout.
Injury with insult added—trial of our cursing powers—
Cursed and cursing back enough to damn a dozen worlds like ours.

'Take my combs down to the grinder, will yer?' 'Seen my cattle-pup?'
'There's a sheep fell down in my shoot—just jump down and pick it up.'

'Give the office when the boss comes.' 'Catch that gory sheep, old man.'
'Count the sheep in my pen, will yer?' 'Fetch my combs back when yer can.'
'When yer get a chance, old feller, will yer pop down to the hut?'
'Fetch my pipe—the cook'll show yer—and I'll let yer have a cut.'

Shearer yells for tar and needle. Ringer's roaring like a bull:
'Wool away, you (son of angels). Where the hell's the (foundling) WOOL!!'
. . . .
Pound a week and station prices—mustn't kick against the pricks—
Seven weeks of lurid mateship—ruined soul and four pounds six.
. . . .
What's that? waiter? *me?* stuffed mutton! Look here, waiter, to be brief,
I said beef! you blood-stained villain! Beef—moo-cow—Roast Bullock—
BEEF!

THE MAN FROM WATERLOO

(With kind regards to "Banjo.")

It was the Man from Waterloo,
When work in town was slack,
Who took the track as bushmen do,
And humped his swag out back.
He tramped for months without a bob,
For most the sheds were full,
Until at last he got a job
At picking up the wool.
He found the work was rather rough,
But swore to see it through,
For he was made of sterling stuff—
The Man from Waterloo.

The first remark was like a stab
That fell his ear upon,
'Twas—'There's another something scab
'The boss has taken on!'
They couldn't let the towny be—
They sneered like anything;
They'd mock him when he'd sound the 'g'
In words that end in 'ing.'

There came a man from Ironbark,
And at the shed he shore;
He scoffed his victuals like a shark,
And like a fiend he swore.
He'd shorn his flowing beard that day—
He found it hard to reap—
Because 'twas hot and in the way
While he was shearing sheep.
His loaded fork in grimy holt
Was poised, his jaws moved fast,
Impatient till his throat could bolt
The mouthful taken last.
He couldn't stand a something toff,
Much less a jackaroo;
And swore to take the trimmings off
The Man from Waterloo.

The towny saw he must be up
Or else be underneath,
And so one day, before them all,
He dared to clean his teeth.

The men came running from the shed,
And shouted, 'Here's a lark!'
'It's gone to clean its tooties!' said
The man from Ironbark.
His feeble joke was much enjoyed;
He sneered as bullies do,
And with a scrubbing-brush he guyed
The Man from Waterloo.

The Jackaroo made no remark
But peeled and waded in,
And soon the Man from Ironbark
Had three teeth less to grin!
And when they knew that he could fight
They swore to see him through,
Because they saw that he was right—
The Man from Waterloo.

Now in a shop in Sydney, near
The Bottle on the Shelf,
The tale is told—with trimmings—by
The Jackaroo himself.
'They made my life a hell,' he said;
'They wouldn't let me be;
'They set the bully of the shed
'To take it out of me.

'The dirt was on him like a sheath,
'He seldom washed his phiz;
'He sneered because I cleaned my teeth—
'I guess I dusted his!
'I treated them as they deserved—
'I signed on one or two!
'They won't forget me soon,' observed
The Man from Waterloo.

SAINT PETER

NOW, I think there is a likeness
'Twixt St. Peter's life and mine,
For he did a lot of trampin'
Long ago in Palestine.
He was 'union' when the workers
First began to organise,
And—I'm glad that old St. Peter
Keeps the gate of Paradise.

When the ancient agitator
And his brothers carried swags,
I've no doubt he very often
Tramped with empty tucker-bags;
And I'm glad he's Heaven's picket,
For I hate explainin' things,
And he'll think a union ticket
Just as good as Whitely King's.

He denied the Saviour's union,
Which was weak of him, no doubt;
But perhaps his feet was blistered
And his boots had given out.
And the bitter storm was rushin'
On the bark and on the slabs,
And a cheerful fire was blazin',
And the hut was full of 'scabs.'
. . . .
When I reach the great head-station—
Which is somewhere 'off the track'—
I won't want to talk with angels
Who have never been out back;
They might bother me with offers
Of a banjo—meanin' well—
And a pair of wings to fly with,
When I only want a spell.

I'll just ask for old St. Peter,
And I think, when he appears,
I will only have to tell him
That I carried swag for years.
'I've been on the track,' I'll tell him,

'An' I done the best I could,'
And he'll understand me better
Than the other angels would.

He won't try to get a chorus
Out of lungs that's worn to rags,
Or to graft the wings on shoulders
That is stiff with humpin' swags.
But I'll rest about the station
Where the work-bell never rings,
Till they blow the final trumpet
And the Great Judge sees to things.

THE STRANGER'S FRIEND

THE strangest things, and the maddest things, that a man can do or say,
To the chaps and fellers and coves Out Back are matters of every day;
Maybe on account of the lives they lead, or the life that their hearts discard—
But never a fool can be too mad or a 'hard case' be too hard.

I met him in Bourke in the Union days—with which we have nought to do
(Their creed was narrow, their methods crude, but they stuck to 'the cause' like glue).
He came into town from the Lost Soul Run for his grim half-yearly 'bend,'
And because of a curious hobby he had, he was known as 'The Stranger's Friend.'

It is true to the region of adjectives when I say that the spree was 'grim,'
For to go on the spree was a sacred rite, or a heathen rite, to him,
To shout for the travellers passing through to the land where the lost soul bakes—
Till they all seemed devils of different breeds, and his pockets were filled with snakes.

In the joyful mood, in the solemn mood—in his cynical stages too—
In the maudlin stage, in the fighting stage, in the stage when all was blue—
From the joyful hour when his spree commenced, right through to the awful end,
He never lost grip of his 'fixed idee' that he was the Stranger's Friend.

'The feller as knows, *he* can battle around for his bloomin' self,' he'd say—
'I don't give a curse for the "blanks" I know—send the hard-up bloke this way;
Send the stranger round, and I'll see him through,' and, e'en as the bushman spoke,
The chaps and fellers would tip the wink to a casual, 'hard-up bloke.'

And it wasn't only a bushman's 'bluff' to the fame of the Friend they scored,
For he'd shout the stranger a suit of clothes, and he'd pay for the stranger's board—
The worst of it was that he'd skite all night on the edge of the stranger's bunk,
And never got helplessly drunk himself till he'd got the stranger drunk.

And the chaps and the fellers would speculate—by way of a ghastly joke—
As to who'd be caught by the 'jim-jams' first?—the Friend or the hard-up bloke?
And the 'Joker' would say that there wasn't a doubt as to who'd be damned in the end,
When the Devil got hold of a hard-up bloke in the shape of the Stranger's Friend.

It mattered not to the Stranger's Friend what the rest might say or think,
He always held that the hard-up state was due to the curse of drink,
To the evils of cards, and of company: 'But a young cove's built that way,
And I was a bloomin' fool meself when I started out,' he'd say.

At the end of the spree, in clean white 'moles,' clean-shaven, and cool as ice,
He'd give the stranger a 'bob' or two, and some straight Out Back advice;
Then he'd tramp away for the Lost Soul Run, where the hot dust rose like smoke,
Having done his duty to all mankind, for he'd 'stuck to a hard-up bloke.'

They'll say 'tis a 'song of a sot,' perhaps, but the Song of a Sot is true.
I have 'battled' myself, and *you* know, you chaps, what a man in the bush goes through;
Let us hope when the last of his sprees is past, and his cheques and his strength are done,
That, amongst the sober and thrifty mates, the Stranger's Friend has *one*.

THE GOD-FORGOTTEN ELECTION

PAT M'DURMER brought the tidings to the town of God-Forgotten:
'There are lively days before ye—commin Parlymint's dissolved!'
And the boys were all excited, for the State, of course, was 'rotten,'
And, in subsequent elections, God-Forgotten was involved.
There was little there to live for save in drinking beer and eating;
But we rose on this occasion ere the news appeared in print,
For the boys of God-Forgotten, at a wild, uproarious meeting,
Nominated Billy Blazes for the commin Parlymint.

Other towns had other favourites, but the day before the battle
Bushmen flocked to God-Forgotten, and the distant sheds were still;
Sheep were left to go to glory, and neglected mobs of cattle
Went a-straying down the river at their sweet bucolic will.
William Spouter stood for Freetrade (and his votes were split by Nottin),
He had influence behind him and he also had the tin,
But across the lonely flatlands came the cry of God-Forgotten,
'Vote for Blazes and Protection, and the land you're living in!'

Pat M'Durmer said, 'Ye schaymers, please to shut yer ugly faces,
Lend yer dirty ears a momint while I give ye all a hint:
Keep ye sober till to-morrow and record yer vote for Blazes
If ye want to send a ringer to the commin Parlymint.
'As a young and growin' township God-Forgotten's been neglected,
And, if we'd be ripresinted, *now's* the moment to begin—
Have the local towns encouraged, local industries purtected:
Vote for Blazes, and Protection, and the land ye're livin' in.

'I don't say that William Blazes is a perfect out-an' outer,
I don't say he have the larnin', for he never had the luck;
I don't say he have the logic, or the gift of gab, like Spouter,
I don't say he have the practice—BUT I SAY HE HAVE THE PLUCK!
Now the country's gone to ruin, and the Governments are rotten,
But he'll save the public credit and purtect the public tin;
To the iverlastin' glory of the name of God-Forgotten
Vote for Blazes and Protection, and the land ye're livin' in!'

Pat M'D. went on the war-path, and he worked like salts and senna,
For he organised committees full of energy and push;
And those wild committees riding through the whisky-fed Gehenna
Routed out astonished voters from their humpies in the bush.
Everything on wheels was 'rinted,' and half-sobered drunks were shot in;

Said M'Durmer to the driver, 'If ye want to save yer skin,
Never stop to wet yer whistles—drive like hell to God-Forgotten,
Make the villains plump for Blazes, and the land they're livin' in.'

Half the local long-departed (for the purpose resurrected)
Plumped for Blazes and Protection, and the country where they died;
So he topped the poll by sixty, and when Blazes was elected
There was victory and triumph on the God-Forgotten side.
Then the boys got up a banquet, and our chairman, Pat M'Durmer,
Was next day discovered sleeping in the local baker's bin—
All the dough had risen round him, but we heard a smothered murmur,
'Vote for Blazes—and Protection—and the land ye're livin' in.'

Now the great Sir William Blazes lives in London, 'cross the waters,
And they say his city mansion is the swellest in West End,
But I very often wonder if his toney sons and daughters
Ever heard of Billy Blazes who was once the 'people's friend.'
Does his biassed memory linger round that wild electioneering
When the men of God-Forgotten stuck to him through thick and thin?
Does he ever, in his dreaming, hear the cry above the cheering:
'Vote for Blazes and Protection, and the land you're livin' in?'
. . . .
Ah, the bush was grand in those days, and the Western boys were daisies,
And their scheming and their dodging would outdo the wildest print;
Still my recollection lingers round the time when Billy Blazes
Was returned by God-Forgotten to the 'Commin Parlymint':
Still I keep a sign of canvas—'twas a mate of mine that made it—
And its paint is cracked and powdered, and its threads are bare and thin,
Yet upon its grimy surface you can read in letters faded:
'Vote for Blazes and Protection, and the Land you're livin' in.'

THE BOSS'S BOOTS

THE shearers squint along the pens, they squint along the 'shoots;'
The shearers squint along the board to catch the Boss's boots;
They have no time to straighten up, they have no time to stare,
But when the Boss is looking on, they like to be aware.

The 'rouser' has no soul to save. Condemn the rouseabout!
And sling 'em in, and rip 'em through, and get the bell-sheep out;
And skim it by the tips at times, or take it with the roots—
But 'pink' 'em nice and pretty when you see the Boss's boots.

The shearing super sprained his foot, as bosses sometimes do—
And wore, until the shed cut out, one 'side-spring' and one shoe;
And though he changed his pants at times—some worn-out and some neat—
No 'tiger' there could possibly mistake the Boss's feet.

The Boss affected larger boots than many Western men,
And Jim the Ringer swore the shoe was half as big again;
And tigers might have *heard* the boss ere any harm was done—
For when he passed it was a sort of dot and carry one.

But now there comes a picker-up who sprained his ankle, too,
And limping round the shed he found the Boss's cast-off shoe.
He went to work, all legs and arms, as green-hand rousers will,
And never dreamed of Boss's boots—much less of Bogan Bill.

Ye sons of sin that tramp and shear in hot and dusty scrubs,
Just keep away from 'headin' 'em,' and keep away from pubs,
And keep away from handicaps—for so your sugar scoots—
And you may own a station yet and wear the Boss's boots.

And Bogan by his mate was heard to mutter through his hair:
'The Boss has got a rat to-day: he's buckin' everywhere—
He's trainin' for a bike, I think, the way he comes an' scoots,
He's like a bloomin' cat on mud the way he shifts his boots.'

Now Bogan Bill was shearing rough and chanced to cut a teat;
He stuck his leg in front at once, and slewed the ewe a bit;
He hurried up to get her through, when, close beside his shoot,
He saw a large and ancient shoe, in mateship with a boot.

He thought that he'd be fined all right—he couldn't turn the 'yoe;'
The more he wished the boss away, the more he wouldn't go;
And Bogan swore amenfully—beneath his breath he swore—
And he was never known to 'pink' so prettily before.

And Bogan through his bristling scalp in his mind's eye could trace,
The cold, sarcastic smile that lurked about the Boss's face;
He cursed him with a silent curse in language known to few,
He cursed him from his boot right up, and then down to his shoe.

But while he shore so mighty clean, and while he screened the teat,
He fancied there was something wrong about the Boss's feet:
The boot grew unfamiliar, and the odd shoe seemed awry,
And slowly up the trouser went the tail of Bogan's eye.

Then swiftly to the features from a plaited green-hide belt—
You'd have to ring a shed or two to feel as Bogan felt—
For 'twas his green-hand picker-up (who wore a vacant look),
And Bogan saw the Boss outside consulting with his cook.

And Bogan Bill was hurt and mad to see that rouseabout;
And Bogan laid his 'Wolseley' down and knocked that rouser out;
He knocked him right across the board, he tumbled through the shoot—
'I'll learn the fool,' said Bogan Bill, 'to flash the Boss's boot!'

The rouser squints along the pens, he squints along the shoots,
And gives his men the office when they miss the Boss's boots.
They have no time to straighten up, they're too well-bred to stare,
But when the Boss is looking on they like to be aware.

The rouser has no soul to lose—it's blarst the rouseabout!
And rip 'em through and yell for 'tar' and get the bell-sheep out,
And take it with the scum at times or take it with the roots,—
But 'pink' 'em nice and pretty when you see the Boss's boots.

'Rouseabout' and 'picker-up' are interchangeable terms in above rhymes, as also 'boss' and 'super'; the shed-name for the latter is 'Boss-over-the-board.' The shearer is paid by the hundred, the rouser by the week. 'Pink 'em pretty': to shear clean to the skin. 'Bell-sheep': shearers are not supposed to take another sheep out of pen when 'Smoke-ho,' breakfast or dinner bell goes, but some time themselves to get so many sheep out, and *one as the bell goes*, which makes more work for the rouser and entrenches on his 'smoke-ho,' as he must leave his 'board' clean. Shearers are seldom or never fined now.

THE CAPTAIN OF THE PUSH

AS the night was falling slowly down on city, town and bush,
From a slum in Jones' Alley sloped the Captain of the Push;
And he scowled towards the North, and he scowled towards the South,
As he hooked his little finger in the corners of his mouth.
Then his whistle, loud and shrill, woke the echoes of the 'Rocks,'
And a dozen ghouls came sloping round the corners of the blocks.

There was nought to rouse their anger; yet the oath that each one swore
Seemed less fit for publication than the one that went before.
For they spoke the gutter language with the easy flow that comes
Only to the men whose childhood knew the brothels and the slums.
Then they spat in turns, and halted; and the one that came behind,
Spitting fiercely on the pavement, called on Heaven to strike him blind.

Let us first describe the captain, bottle-shouldered, pale and thin,
For he was the beau-ideal of a Sydney larrikin;
E'en his hat was most suggestive of the city where we live,
With a gallows-tilt that no one, save a larrikin, can give;
And the coat, a little shorter than the writer would desire,
Showed a more or less uncertain portion of his strange attire.

That which tailors know as 'trousers'—known by him as 'bloomin' bags'—
Hanging loosely from his person, swept, with tattered ends, the flags;
And he had a pointed sternpost to the boots that peeped below
(Which he laced up from the centre of the nail of his great toe),
And he wore his shirt uncollar'd, and the tie correctly wrong;
But I think his vest was shorter than should be in one so long.

And the captain crooked his finger at a stranger on the kerb,
Whom he qualified politely with an adjective and verb,
And he begged the Gory Bleeders that they wouldn't interrupt
Till he gave an introduction—it was painfully abrupt—
'Here's the bleedin' push, me covey—here's a (something) from the bush!
Strike me dead, he wants to join us!' said the captain of the push.

Said the stranger: 'I am nothing but a bushy and a dunce;
But I read about the Bleeders in the WEEKLY GASBAG once:
Sitting lonely in the humpy when the wind began to "whoosh,"
How I longed to share the dangers and the pleasures of the push!
Gosh! I hate the swells and good 'uns—I could burn 'em in their beds;
I am with you, if you'll have me, and I'll break their blazing heads.'

'Now, look here,' exclaimed the captain to the stranger from the bush,
'Now, look here—suppose a feller was to split upon the push,
Would you lay for him and fetch him, even if the traps were round?
Would you lay him out and kick him to a jelly on the ground?
Would you jump upon the nameless—kill, or cripple him, or both?
Speak? or else I'll—SPEAK!' The stranger answered, 'My kerlonial oath!'

'Now, look here,' exclamed the captain to the stranger from the bush,
'Now, look here—suppose the Bleeders let you come and join the push,
Would you smash a bleedin' bobby if you got the blank alone?
Would you break a swell or Chinkie—split his garret with a stone?
Would you have a "moll" to keep yer—like to swear off work for good?'
'Yes, my oath!' replied the stranger. 'My kerlonial oath! I would!'

'Now, look here,' exclamed the captain to that stranger from the bush,
'Now, look here—before the Bleeders let yer come and join the push,
You must prove that you're a blazer—you must prove that you have grit
Worthy of a Gory Bleeder—you must show your form a bit—
Take a rock and smash that winder?' and the stranger, nothing loth,
Took the rock and—smash! They only muttered 'My kerlonial oath!'

So they swore him in, and found him sure of aim and light of heel,
And his only fault, if any, lay in his excessive zeal;
He was good at throwing metal, but we chronicle with pain
That he jumped upon a victim, damaging the watch and chain,
Ere the Bleeders had secured them; yet the captain of the push
Swore a dozen oaths in favour of the stranger from the bush.

Late next morn the captain, rising, hoarse and thirsty from his lair,
Called the newly-feather'd Bleeder, but the stranger wasn't there!
Quickly going through the pockets of his 'bloomin' bags,' he learned
That the stranger had been through him for the stuff his 'moll' had earned;
And the language that he muttered I should scarcely like to tell
(Stars! and notes of exclamation!! blank and dash will do as well).

In the night the captain's signal woke the echoes of the 'Rocks,'
Brought the Gory Bleeders sloping thro' the shadows of the blocks;
And they swore the stranger's action was a blood-escaping shame,
While they waited for the nameless, but the nameless never came.
And the Bleeders soon forgot him; but the captain of the push
Still is 'laying' round, in ballast, for the nameless 'from the bush.'

BILLY'S 'SQUARE AFFAIR'

LONG BILL, the captain of the push, was tired of his estate,
And wished to change his life and win the love of something 'straight';
'Twas rumour'd that the Gory B.'s had heard Long Bill declare
That he would turn respectable and wed a 'square affair.'

He craved the kiss of innocence; his spirit longed to rise;
The 'Crimson Streak,' his faithful 'piece,' grew hateful in his eyes;
(And though, in her entirety, the Crimson Streak 'was there,'
I grieve to state the Crimson Streak was not a 'square affair.')

He wanted clothes, a masher suit, he wanted boots and hat;
His girl had earned a quid or two—he wouldn't part with that;
And so he went to Brickfield Hill, and from a draper there
He 'shook' the proper kind of togs to fetch a 'square affair.'

Long Bill went to the barber's shop and had a shave and singe,
And from his narrow forehead combed his darling Mabel fringe;
Long Bill put on a 'square cut' and he brushed his boots with care,
And roved about the Gardens till he mashed a 'square affair.'

She was a tony servant-girl from somewhere on 'the Shore;'
She dressed in style that suited Bill—he could not wish for more.
While in her guileless presence he had ceased to chew or swear,
He knew the kind of barrack that can fetch a square affair.

To thus desert his donah old was risky and a sin,
And 'twould have served him right if she had caved his garret in.
The Gory Bleeders thought it too, and warned him to take care
In case the Crimson Streak got scent of Billy's square affair.

He took her to the stalls; 'twas dear, but Billy said 'Wot odds!'
He couldn't take his square affair amongst the crimson gods.
They wandered in the park at night, and hugged each other there—
But, ah! the Crimson Streak got wind of Billy's square affair!

'The blank and space and stars!' she yelled; 'the nameless crimson dash!
I'll smash the blanky crimson and his square affair, I'll smash'—
In short, she drank and raved and shrieked and tore her crimson hair,
And swore to murder Billy and to pound his square affair.

And so one summer evening, as the day was growing dim,
She watched her bloke go out, and foxed his square affair and him.
That night the park was startled by the shrieks that rent the air—
The 'Streak' had gone for Billy and for Billy's square affair.

The 'gory' push had foxed the Streak, they foxed her to the park,
And they, of course, were close at hand to see the bleedin' lark;
A cop arrived in time to hear a 'gory B.' declare
Gor blar-me! here's the Red Streak foul of Billy's square affair.'
. . . .
Now Billy scowls about the Rocks, his manly beauty marr'd,
And Billy's girl, upon her 'ed, is doin' six months 'ard;
Bill's swivel eye is in a sling, his heart is in despair,
And in the Sydney 'Orspital lies Billy's square affair.

A DERRY ON A COVE

'Twas in the felon's dock he stood, his eyes were black and blue;
His voice with grief was broken, and his nose was broken, too;
He muttered, as that broken nose he wiped upon his cap—
'It's orful when the p'leece has got a derry on a chap.

'I am a honest workin' cove, as any bloke can see,
It's just because the p'leece has got a derry, sir, on me;
Oh, yes, the legal gents can grin, I say it ain't no joke—
It's cruel when the p'leece has got a derry on a bloke.'

'Why don't you go to work?' he said (he muttered, 'Why don't you?').
'Yer honer knows as well as me there ain't no work to do.
And when I try to find a job I'm shaddered by a trap—
It's awful when the p'leece has got a derry on a chap.'

I sigh'd and shed a tearlet for that noble nature marred,
But, ah! the Bench was rough on him, and gave him six months' hard.
He only said, 'Beyond the grave you'll cop it hot, by Jove!
There ain't no angel p'leece to get a derry on a cove.'

RISE YE! RISE YE!

RISE ye! rise ye! noble toilers! claim your rights with fire and steel!
Rise ye! for the cursed tyrants crush ye with the hiron 'eel!
They would treat ye worse than sl-a-a-ves! they would treat ye worse than brutes!
Rise and crush the selfish tyrants! ku-r-rush them with your hob-nailed boots!
Rise ye! rise ye! glorious toilers!
Rise ye! rise ye! noble toilers!
Erwake! er-rise!

Rise ye! rise ye! noble toilers! tyrants come across the waves!
Will ye yield the Rights of Labour? will ye? *will* ye still be sl-a-a-ves?!!!
Rise ye! rise ye! mighty toilers! and revoke the rotten laws!
Lo! your wives go out a-washing while ye battle for the caws!
Rise ye! rise ye! glorious toilers!
Rise ye! rise ye! noble toilers!
Erwake! er-rise!

Our gerlorious dawn is breaking! Lo! the tyrant trembles now!
He will sta-a-rve us here no longer! toilers will not bend or bow!
Rise ye! rise ye! noble toilers! rise! behold, revenge is near;
See the leaders of the people! come an' 'ave a pint o' beer!
Rise ye! rise ye! noble toilers!
Rise ye! rise ye! glorious toilers!
Erwake! er-rise!

Lo! the poor are starved, my brothers! lo! our wives and children weep!
Lo! our women toil to keep us while the toilers are asleep!
Rise ye! rise ye! noble toilers! rise and break the tyrant's chain!
March ye! march ye! mighty toilers! even to the battle plain!
Rise ye! rise ye! noble toilers!
Rise ye! rise ye! noble toilers!
Erwake! er-r-rise!

THE BALLAD OF MABEL CLARE

YE children of the Land of Gold,
I sing a song to you,
And if the jokes are somewhat old,
The main idea's new.
So be it sung, by hut and tent,
Where tall the native grows;
And understand, the song is meant
For singing through the nose.

There dwelt a hard old cockatoo
On western hills far out,
Where everything is green and blue,
Except, of course, in drought;
A crimson Anarchist was he—
Held other men in scorn—
Yet preached that ev'ry man was free,
And also 'ekal born.'

He lived in his ancestral hut—
His missus wasn't there—
And there was no one with him but
His daughter, Mabel Clare.
Her eyes and hair were like the sun;
Her foot was like a mat;
Her cheeks a trifle overdone;
She was a democrat.

A manly independence, born
Among the trees, she had,
She treated womankind with scorn,
And often cursed her dad.
She hated swells and shining lights,
For she had seen a few,
And she believed in 'women's rights'
(She mostly got 'em, too).

A stranger at the neighb'ring run
Sojourned, the squatter's guest,
He was unknown to anyone,
But like a swell was dress'd;
He had an eyeglass to his eye,

A collar to his ears,
His feet were made to tread the sky,
His mouth was formed for sneers.

He wore the latest toggery,
The loudest thing in ties—
'Twas generally reckoned he
Was something in disguise.
But who he was, or whence he came,
Was long unknown, except
Unto the squatter, who the name
And noble secret kept.

And strolling in the noontide heat,
Beneath the blinding glare,
This noble stranger chanced to meet
The radiant Mabel Clare.
She saw at once he was a swell—
According to her lights—
But, ah! 'tis very sad to tell,
She met him oft of nights.

And, strolling through a moonlit gorge,
She chatted all the while
Of Ingersoll, and Henry George,
And Bradlaugh and Carlyle:
In short, he learned to love the girl,
And things went on like this,
Until he said he was an Earl,
And asked her to be his.

'Oh, say no more, Lord Kawlinee,
Oh, say no more!' she said;
'Oh, say no more, Lord Kawlinee,
I wish that I was dead;
My head is in a hawful whirl,
The truth I dare not tell—
I am a democratic girl,
And cannot wed a swell!'

'Oh love!' he cried, 'but you forget
That you are most unjust;
'Twas not my fault that I was set

Within the upper crust.
Heed not the yarns the poets tell—
Oh, darling, do not doubt
A simple lord can love as well
As any rouseabout!

'For you I'll give my fortune up—
I'd go to work for you!
I'll put the money in the cup
And drop the title, too.
Oh, fly with me! Oh, fly with me
Across the mountains blue!
Hoh, fly with me! *Hoh, fly with me!*———'
That very night she flew.

They took the train and journeyed down—
Across the range they sped—
Until they came to Sydney town,
Where shortly they were wed.
And still upon the western wild
Admiring teamsters tell
How Mabel's father cursed his child
For clearing with a swell.

'What ails my bird this bridal night,'
Exclaimed Lord Kawlinee;
'What ails my own this bridal night—
O love, confide in me!'
'Oh now,' she said, 'that I am yaws
You'll let me weep—I must—
I did desert the people's cause
To join the upper crust.'

O proudly smiled his lordship then—
His chimney-pot he floor'd—
'Look up, my love, and smile again,
For I am not a lord!'
His eye-glass from his eye he tore,
The dickey from his breast,
And turned and stood his bride before
A rouseabout—confess'd!

'Unknown I've loved you long,' he said,
'And I have loved you true—
A-shearing in your guv'ner's shed
I learned to worship you.
I do not care for place or pelf,
For now, my love, I'm sure
That you will love me for myself
And not because I'm poor.

'To prove your love I spent my cheque
To buy this swell rig-out;
So fling your arms about my neck
For I'm a rouseabout!'
At first she gave a startled cry,
Then, safe from care's alarms,
She sigh'd a soul-subduing sigh
And sank into his arms.

He pawned the togs, and home he took
His bride in all her charms;
The proud old cockatoo received
The pair with open arms.
And long they lived, the faithful bride,
The noble rouseabout—
And if she wasn't satisfied
She never let it out.

CONSTABLE M'CARTY'S INVESTIGATIONS

MOST unpleasantly adjacent to the haunts of lower orders
Stood a 'terrace' in the city when the current year began,
And a notice indicated there were vacancies for boarders
In the middle house, and lodgings for a single gentleman.
Now, a singular observer could have seen but few attractions
Whether in the house, or 'missus, or the notice, or the street,
But at last there came a lodger whose appearances and actions
Puzzled Constable M'Carty, the policeman on the beat.

He (the single gent) was wasted almost to emaciation,
And his features were the palest that M'Carty ever saw,
And these indications, pointing to a past of dissipation,
Greatly strengthened the suspicions of the agent of the law.
He (the lodger—hang the pronoun!) seemed to like the stormy weather,
When the elements in battle kept it up a little late;
Yet he'd wander in the moonlight when the stars were close together,
Taking ghostly consolation in a visionary state.

He would walk the streets at midnight, when the storm-king raised his banner,
Walk without his old umbrella,—wave his arms above his head:
Or he'd fold them tight, and mutter, in a wild, disjointed manner,
While the town was wrapped in slumber and he should have been in bed.
Said the constable-on-duty: 'Shure, Oi wonther phwat his trade is?'
And the constable would watch him from the shadow of a wall,
But he never picked a pocket, and he ne'er accosted ladies,
And the constable was puzzled what to make of him at all.

Now, M'Carty had arrested more than one notorious dodger,
He had heard of men afflicted with the strangest kind of fads,
But he couldn't fix the station or the business of the lodger,
Who at times would chum with cadgers, and at other times with cads.
And the constable would often stand and wonder how the gory
Sheol the stranger got his living, for he loafed the time away
And he often sought a hillock when the sun went down in glory,
Just as if he was a mourner at the burial of the day.

Mac. had noticed that the lodger did a mighty lot of smoking,
And could 'stow away a long 'un,' never winking, so he could;
And M'Carty once, at midnight, came upon the lodger poking
Round about suspicious alleys where the common houses stood.

Yet the constable had seen him in a class above suspicion—
Seen him welcomed with effusion by a dozen 'toney gents'—
Seen him driving in the buggy of a rising politician
Thro' the gateway of the member's toney private residence.

And the constable, off duty, had observed the lodger slipping
Down a lane to where the river opened on the ocean wide,
Where he'd stand for hours gazing at the distant anchor'd shipping,
But he never took his coat off, so it wasn't suicide.
For the constable had noticed that a man who's filled with loathing
For his selfish fellow-creatures and the evil things that be,
Will, for some mysterious reason, shed a portion of his clothing,
Ere he takes his first and final plunge into eternity.

And M'Carty, once at midnight—be it said to his abasement—
Left his beat and climbed a railing of considerable height,
Just to watch the lodger's shadow on the curtain of his casement
While the little room was lighted in the listening hours of night.
Now, at first the shadow hinted that the substance sat inditing;
Now it indicated toothache, or the headache; and again,
'Twould exaggerate the gestures of a dipsomaniac fighting
Those original conceptions of a whisky-sodden brain.

Then the constable, retreating, scratched his head and muttered 'Sorra
Wan of me can undershtand it. But Oi'll keep me Oi on him,
Divil take him and his tantrums; he's a lunatic, begorra!
Or, if he was up to mischief, he'd be sure to douse the glim.'
But M'Carty wasn't easy, for he had a vague suspicion
That a 'skame' was being plotted; and he thought the matter down
Till his mind was pretty certain that the business was sedition,
And the man, in league with others, sought to overthrow the Crown.

But, in spite of observation, Mac. received no information
And was forced to stay inactive, being puzzled for a charge.
That the lodger was a madman seemed the only explanation,
Tho' the house would scarcely harbour such a lunatic at large.
His appearance failed to warrant apprehension as a vagrant,
Tho' 'twas getting very shabby, as the constable could see;
But M'Carty in the meantime hoped to catch him in a flagrant
Breach of peace, or the intention to commit a felony.

(For digression there is leisure, and it is the writer's pleasure
Just to pause a while and ponder on a painful legal fact,

Being forced to say in sorrow, and a line of doubtful measure,
That there's nothing so elastic as the cruel Vagrant Act)
Now, M'Carty knew his duty, and was brave as any lion,
But he dreaded being 'landed' in an influential bog—
As the chances were he would be if the man he had his eye on
Was a person of importance who was travelling *incog*.

Want of sleep and over-worry seemed to tell upon M'Carty:
He was thirsty more than ever, but his appetite resigned;
He was previously reckoned as a jolly chap and hearty,
But the mystery was lying like a mountain on his mind.
Tho' he tried his best, he couldn't get a hold upon the lodger,
For the latter's antecedents weren't known to the police—
They considered that the 'devil' was a dark and artful dodger
Who was scheming under cover for the downfall of the peace.

'Twas a simple explanation, though M'Carty didn't know it,
Which with half his penetration he might easily have seen,
For the object of his dangerous suspicions was a poet,
Who was not so widely famous as he thought he should have been.
And the constable grew thinner, till one morning, 'little dhramin'
Av the sword of revelation that was leapin' from its sheath,'
He alighted on some verses in the columns of the FRAYMAN,
'*Wid the christian name an' surname av the lodger onderneath!*'

Now, M'Carty and the poet are as brother is to brother,
Or, at least, as brothers should be; and they very often meet
On the lonely block at midnight, and they wink at one another—
Disappearing down the by-way of a shanty in the street.
And the poet's name you're asking?—well, the ground is very tender,
You must wait until the public put the gilt upon the name,
Till a glorious, sorrow-drowning, and, perhaps, a final 'bender,'
Heralds his triumphant entrance to the thunder-halls of Fame.

AT THE TUG-OF-WAR

'Twas in a tug-of-war where I—the guvnor's hope and pride—
Stepped proudly on the platform as the ringer on my side;
Old dad was in his glory there—it gave the old man joy
To fight a passage through the crowd and barrack for his boy.

A friend came up and said to me, 'Put out your muscles, John,
And pull them to eternity—your guvnor's looking on.'
I paused before I grasped the rope, and glanced around the place,
And, foremost in the waiting crowd, I saw the old man's face.

My mates were strong and plucky chaps, but very soon I knew
That our opponents had the weight and strength to pull them through;
The boys were losing surely and defeat was very near,
When, high above the mighty roar, I heard the old man cheer!

I felt my muscles swelling when the old man cheer'd for me,
I felt as though I'd burst my heart, or gain the victory!
I shouted, 'Now! Together!' and a steady strain replied,
And, with a mighty heave, I helped to beat the other side!

Oh! how the old man shouted in his wild, excited joy!
I thought he'd burst his boiler then, a-cheering for his boy;
The chaps, oh! how they cheered me, while the girls all smiled so kind,
They praised me, little dreaming, how the old man pulled behind.
. . . .
He barracks for his boy no more—his grave is old and green,
And sons have grown up round me since he vanished from the scene;
But, when the cause is worthy where I fight for victory,
In fancy still I often hear the old man cheer for me.

HERE'S LUCK!

OLD Time is tramping close to-day—you hear his bluchers fall,
A mighty change is on the way, an' God protect us all;
Some dust'll fly from beery coats—at least it's been declared.
I'm glad that wimin has the votes—but just a trifle scared.

I'm just a trifle scared—For why? The wimin mean to rule;
It makes me feel like days gone by when I was caned at school.
The days of men is nearly dead—of double moons and stars—
They'll soon put out our pipes, 'tis said, an' close the public bars.

No more we'll take a glass of ale when pushed with care an' strife,
An' chuckle home with that old tale we used to tell the wife.
We'll laugh an' joke an' sing no more with jolly beery chums,
An' shout 'Here's luck!' while waitin' for the luck that never comes.

Did we prohibit swillin' tea clean out of common-sense
Or legislate on gossipin' across a backyard fence?
Did we prohibit bustles—or the hoops when they was here?
The wimin never think of this—they want to stop our beer.

The track o' life is dry enough, an' crossed with many a rut,
But, oh! we'll find it long an' rough when all the pubs is shut;
When all the pubs is shut, an' gone the doors we used to seek,
An' we go toilin', thirstin' on through Sundays all the week.

For since the days when pubs was 'inns'—in years gone past 'n' far—
Poor sinful souls have drowned their sins an' sorrers at the bar;
An' though at times it led to crimes, an' debt, and such complaints—
I scarce dare think about the time when all mankind is saints.

'Twould make the bones of Bacchus leap an' break his coffin lid;
And Burns's ghost would wail an' weep as Bobby never did.
But let the preachers preach in style, an' rave and rant—'n' buck,
I rather guess they'll hear awhile the old war-cry: 'Here's Luck!'

The world might wobble round the sun, an' all the banks go bung,
But pipes'll smoke an' liquor run while Auld Lang Syne is sung.
While men are driven through the mill, an' flinty times is struck,
They'll find a private entrance still!
Here's Luck, old man—Here's Luck!

THE MEN WHO COME BEHIND

THERE'S a class of men (and women) who are always on their guard—
Cunning, treacherous, suspicious—feeling softly—grasping hard—
Brainy, yet without the courage to forsake the beaten track—
Cautiously they feel their way behind a bolder spirit's back.

If you save a bit of money, and you start a little store—
Say, an oyster-shop, for instance, where there wasn't one before—
When the shop begins to pay you, and the rent is off your mind,
You will see another started by a chap that comes behind.

So it is, and so it might have been, my friend, with me and you—
When a friend of both and neither interferes between the two;
They will fight like fiends, forgetting in their passion mad and blind,
That the row is mostly started by the folk who come behind.

They will stick to you like sin will, while your money comes and goes,
But they'll leave you when you haven't got a shilling in your clothes.
You may get some help above you, but you'll nearly always find
That you cannot get assistance from the men who come behind.

There are many, far too many, in the world of prose and rhyme,
Always looking for another's 'footsteps on the sands of time.'
Journalistic imitators are the meanest of mankind;
And the grandest themes are hackneyed by the pens that come behind.

If you strike a novel subject, write it up, and do not fail,
They will rhyme and prose about it till your very own is stale,
As they raved about the region that the wattle-boughs perfume
Till the reader cursed the bushman and the stink of wattle-bloom.

They will follow in your footsteps while you're groping for the light;
But they'll run to get before you when they see you're going right;
And they'll trip you up and baulk you in their blind and greedy heat,
Like a stupid pup that hasn't learned to trail behind your feet.

Take your loads of sin and sorrow on more energetic backs!
Go and strike across the country where there are not any tracks!
And—we fancy that the subject could be further treated here,
But we'll leave it to be hackneyed by the fellows in the rear.

THE DAYS WHEN WE WENT SWIMMING

THE breezes waved the silver grass,
Waist-high along the siding,
And to the creek we ne'er could pass
Three boys on bare-back riding;
Beneath the sheoaks in the bend
The waterhole was brimming—
Do you remember yet, old friend,
The times we 'went in swimming?'

The days we 'played the wag' from school—
Joys shared—and paid for singly—
The air was hot, the water cool—
And naked boys are kingly!
With mud for soap the sun to dry—
A well planned lie to stay us,
And dust well rubbed on neck and face
Lest cleanliness betray us.

And you'll remember farmer Kutz—
Though scarcely for his bounty—
He leased a forty-acre block,
And thought he owned the county;
A farmer of the old world school,
That men grew hard and grim in,
He drew his water from the pool
That we preferred to swim in.

And do you mind when down the creek
His angry way he wended,
A green-hide cartwhip in his hand
For our young backs intended?
Three naked boys upon the sand—
Half buried and half sunning—
Three startled boys without their clothes
Across the paddocks running.

We've had some scares, but we looked blank
When, resting there and chumming,
One glanced by chance along the bank
And saw the farmer coming!
And home impressions linger yet

Of cups of sorrow brimming;
I hardly think that we'll forget
The last day we went swimming.

THE OLD BARK SCHOOL

It was built of bark and poles, and the floor was full of holes
Where each leak in rainy weather made a pool;
And the walls were mostly cracks lined with calico and sacks—
There was little need for windows in the school.

Then we rode to school and back by the rugged gully track,
On the old grey horse that carried three or four;
And he looked so very wise that he lit the master's eyes
Every time he put his head in at the door.

He had run with Cobb and Co.—'that grey leader, let him go!'
There were men 'as knowed the brand upon his hide,'
And 'as knowed it on the course'. Funeral service: 'Good old horse!'
When we burnt him in the gully where he died.

And the master thought the same. 'Twas from Ireland that he came,
Where the tanks are full all summer, and the feed is simply grand;
And the joker then in vogue said his lessons wid a brogue—
'Twas unconscious imitation, let the reader understand.

And we learnt the world in scraps from some ancient dingy maps
Long discarded by the public-schools in town;
And as nearly every book dated back to Captain Cook
Our geography was somewhat upside-down.

It was 'in the book' and so—well, at that we'd let it go,
For we never would believe that print could lie;
And we all learnt pretty soon that when we came out at noon
'The sun is in the south part of the sky.'

And Ireland! *that* was known from the coast line to Athlone:
We got little information *re* the land that gave us birth;
Save that Captain Cook was killed (and was very likely grilled)
And 'the natives of New Holland are the lowest race on earth.'

And a woodcut, in its place, of the same degraded race
Seemed a lot more like a camel than the black-fellows we knew;
Jimmy Bullock, with the rest, scratched his head and gave it best;
But his faith was sadly shaken by a bobtailed kangaroo.

But the old bark-school is gone, and the spot it stood upon
Is a cattle-camp in winter where the curlew's cry is heard;
There's a brick-school on the flat, but a schoolmate teaches that,
For, about the time they built it, our old master was 'transferred.'

But the bark-school comes again with exchanges 'cross the plain—
With the OUT-BACK ADVERTISER; and my fancy roams at large
When I read of passing stock, of a western mob or flock,
With 'James Bullock,' 'Grey,' or 'Henry Dale' in charge.

And I think how Jimmy went from the old bark school content,
With his 'eddication' finished, with his pack-horse after him;
And perhaps if I were back I would take the self-same track,
For I wish my learning ended when the Master 'finished' Jim.

TROUBLE ON THE SELECTION

You lazy boy, you're here at last,
You must be wooden-legged
Now, are you sure the gate is fast
And all the sliprails pegged
And all the milkers at the yard,
The calves all in the pen?
We don't want Poley's calf to suck
His mother dry again.

And did you mend the broken rail
And make it firm and neat?
I s'pose you want that brindle steer
All night among the wheat.
And if he finds the lucerne patch,
He'll stuff his belly full;
He'll eat till he gets 'blown' on that
And busts like Ryan's bull.

Old Spot is lost? You'll drive me mad,
You will, upon my soul!
She might be in the boggy swamps
Or down a digger's hole.
You needn't talk, you never looked
You'd find her if you'd choose,
Instead of poking 'possum logs
And hunting kangaroos.

How came your boots as wet as muck?
You tried to drown the ants!
Why don't you take your bluchers off,
Good Lord, he's tore his pants!
Your father's coming home to-night;
You'll catch it hot, you'll see.
Now go and wash your filthy face
And come and get your tea.

THE PROFESSIONAL WANDERER

When you've knocked about the country—been away from home for years;
When the past, by distance softened, nearly fills your eyes with tears—
You are haunted oft, wherever or however you may roam,
By a fancy that you ought to go and see the folks at home.
You forget the family quarrels—little things that used to jar—
And you think of how they'll worry—how they wonder where you are;
You will think you served them badly, and your own part you'll condemn,
And it strikes you that you'll surely be a novelty to them,
For your voice has somewhat altered, and your face has somewhat changed—
And your views of men and matters over wider fields have ranged.
Then it's time to save your money, or to watch it (how it goes!);
Then it's time to get a 'Gladstone' and a decent suit of clothes;
Then it's time to practise daily with a hair-brush and a comb,
Till you drop in unexpected on the folks and friends at home.

When you've been at home for some time, and the novelty's worn off,
And old chums no longer court you, and your friends begin to scoff;
When 'the girls' no longer kiss you, crying 'Jack! how you have changed!'
When you're stale to your relations, and their manner seems estranged;
When the old domestic quarrels, round the table thrice a day,
Make it too much like the old times—make you wish you'd stayed away,
When, in short, you've spent your money in the fulness of your heart,
And your clothes are getting shabby.... Then it's high time to depart.

A LITTLE MISTAKE

'Tis a yarn I heard of a new-chum 'trap'
On the edge of the Never-Never,
Where the dead men lie and the black men lie,
And the bushman lies for ever.

'Twas the custom still with the local blacks
To cadge in the 'altogether'—
They had less respect for our feelings then,
And more respect for the weather.

The trooper said to the sergeant's wife:
'Sure, I wouldn't seem unpleasant;
But there's women and childer about the place,
And—barrin' a lady's present—

'There's ould King Billy wid niver a stitch
For a month—may the drought cremate him!—
Bar the wan we put in his dhirty head,
Where his old Queen Mary bate him.

'God give her strength!—and a peaceful reign—
Though she flies in a bit av a passion
If ony wan hints that her shtoyle an' luks
Are a trifle behind the fashion.

'There's two of the boys by the stable now—
Be the powers! I'll teach the varmints
To come wid nought but a shirt apiece,
And wid dirt for their nayther garmints.

'Howld on, ye blaggards! How dare ye dare
To come widin sight av the houses?—
I'll give ye a warnin' all for wance
An' a couple of ould pair of trousers.'

They took the pants as a child a toy,
The constable's words beguiling
A smile of something beside their joy;
And they took their departure smiling.

And that very day, when the sun was low,
Two blackfellows came to the station;
They were filled with the courage of Queensland rum
And bursting with indignation.

The constable noticed, with growing ire,
They'd apparently dressed in a hurry;
And their language that day, I am sorry to say,
Mostly consisted of 'plurry.'

The constable heard, and he wished himself back
In the land of the bogs and the ditches—
'You plurry big tight-britches p'liceman, what for
You gibbit our missuses britches?'

And this was a case, I am bound to confess,
Where civilisation went under;
Had one of the gins been *less* modest in dress
He'd never have made such a blunder.

And here let the moral be duly made known,
And hereafter signed and attested:
We should place more reliance on that which is shown
And less upon what is suggested.

A STUDY IN THE "NOOD"

'A SAILOR named Grice was seen by the guard of a goods train lying close to the railway-line near Warner Town (S.A.) in a nude condition. He was unconscious, and had lain there three days, during one of which the glass registed 110 in the shade. *Grice expressed surprise that the train did not pick him up.*'—Daily paper. In consequence, the muse:—

HE was bare—we don't want to be rude—
(His condition was owing to drink)
They say his condition was nood,
Which amounts to the same thing, we think
(We mean his *condition*, we think,
'Twas a naked condition, or *nood*,
Which amounts to the same thing, we think)

Uncovered he lay on the grass
That shrivelled and shrunk; and he stayed
Three hot summer days, while the glass
Was one hundred and ten in the shade.
(We nearly remarked that he *laid*,
But that was bad grammar we thought—
It *does* sound bucolic, we think
It smacks of the barnyard—
Of farming—of *pullets* in short.)

Unheeded he lay on the dirt;
Beside him a part of his dress,
A tattered and threadbare old shirt
Was raised as a flag of distress.
(On a stick, like a flag of distress—
Reversed—we mean that the tail-end was up
Half-mast—on a stick—an evident flag of distress.)

Perhaps in his dreams he persood
Bright visions of heav'nly bliss;
And artists who study the nood
Never saw such a study as this.
The 'luggage' went by and the guard
Looked out and his eyes fell on Grice—
We fancy he looked at him hard,
We think that he looked at him twice.

They say (if the telegram's true)
When he woke up he wondered (good Lord!)
'Why the engine-man didn't heave to—
Why the train didn't take him aboard.'
And now, by the case of poor Grice,
We think that a daily express
Should travel with sunshades and ice,
And a lookout for flags of distress.

A WORD TO TEXAS JACK

TEXAS JACK, you are amusin'. By Lord Harry, how I laughed
When I seen yer rig and saddle with its bulwarks fore-and-aft;
Holy smoke! In such a saddle how the dickens can yer fall?
Why, I seen a gal ride bareback with no bridle on at all!
Gosh! so-help-me! strike-me-balmy! if a bit o' scenery
Like ter you in all yer rig-out on the earth I ever see!
How I'd like ter see a bushman use yer fixins, Texas Jack;
On the remnant of a saddle he can ride to hell and back.
Why, I heerd a mother screamin' when her kid went tossin' by
Ridin' bareback on a bucker that had murder in his eye.

What? yer come to learn the natives how to squat on horse's back!
Learn the cornstalk ridin'! Blazes!—w'at yer giv'n' us, Texas Jack?
Learn the cornstalk—what the flamin', jumptup! where's my country gone?
Why, the cornstalk's mother often rides the day afore he's born!

You may talk about your ridin' in the city, bold an' free,
Talk o' ridin' in the city, Texas Jack, but where'd yer be
When the stock horse snorts an' bunches all 'is quarters in a hump,
And the saddle climbs a sapling, an' the horse-shoes split a stump?

No, before yer teach the native you must ride without a fall
Up a gum or down a gully nigh as steep as any wall—
You must swim the roarin' Darlin' when the flood is at its height
Bearin' down the stock an' stations to the great Australian Bight.

You can't count the bulls an' bisons that yer copped with your lassoo—
But a stout old myall bullock p'raps 'ud learn yer somethin' new;
Yer'd better make yer will an' leave yer papers neat an' trim
Before yer make arrangements for the lassooin' of *him*;
Ere you'n' yer horse is catsmeat, fittin' fate for sich galoots,
And yer saddle's turned to laces like we put in blucher boots.

And yer say yer death on Injins! We've got somethin' in yer line—
If yer think your fitin's ekal to the likes of Tommy Ryan.
Take yer karkass up to Queensland where the allygators chew
And the carpet-snake is handy with his tail for a lassoo;
Ride across the hazy regins where the lonely emus wail
An' ye'll find the black'll track yer while yer lookin' for his trail;
He can track yer without stoppin' for a thousand miles or more—
Come again, and he will show yer where yer spit the year before.

But yer'd best be mighty careful, you'll be sorry you kem here
When yer skewered to the fakements of yer saddle with a spear—
When the boomerang is sailin' in the air, may heaven help yer!
It will cut yer head off goin', an' come back again and skelp yer.

P.S.—As poet and as Yankee I will greet you, Texas Jack,
For it isn't no ill-feelin' that is gettin' up my back,
But I won't see this land crowded by each Yank and British cuss
Who takes it in his head to come a-civilisin' us.

So if you feel like shootin' now, don't let yer pistol cough—
(Our Government is very free at chokin' fellers off);
And though on your great continent there's misery in the towns
An' not a few untitled lords and kings without their crowns,
I will admit your countrymen is busted big, an' free,
An' great on ekal rites of men and great on liberty;
I will admit yer fathers punched the gory tyrant's head,
But then we've got our heroes, too, the diggers that is dead—
The plucky men of Ballarat who toed the scratch right well
And broke the nose of Tyranny and made his peepers swell
For yankin' Lib.'s gold tresses in the roarin' days gone by,
An' doublin' up his dirty fist to black her bonny eye;
So when it comes to ridin' mokes, or hoistin' out the Chow,
Or stickin' up for labour's rights, we don't want showin' how.

They come to learn us cricket in the days of long ago,
An' Hanlan come from Canada to learn us how to row,
An' 'doctors' come from 'Frisco just to learn us how to skite,
An' 'pugs' from all the lands on earth to learn us how to fight;
An' when they go, as like or not, we find we're taken in,
They've left behind no larnin'—but they've carried off our tin.

THE GROG-AN'-GRUMBLE STEEPLECHASE

'Twixt the coastline and the border lay the town of Grog-an'-Grumble
In the days before the bushman was a dull 'n' heartless drudge,
An' they say the local meeting was a drunken rough-and-tumble,
Which was ended pretty often by an inquest on the judge.
An' 'tis said the city talent very often caught a tartar
In the Grog-an'-Grumble sportsman, 'n' retired with broken heads,
For the fortune, life, and safety of the Grog-an'-Grumble starter
Mostly hung upon the finish of the local thoroughbreds.

Pat M'Durmer was the owner of a horse they called the Screamer,
Which he called the 'quickest shtepper 'twixt the Darling and the sea;'
And I think it's very doubtful if the stomach-troubled dreamer
Ever saw a more outrageous piece of equine scenery;
For his points were most decided, from his end to his beginning,
He had eyes of different colour, and his legs they wasn't mates.
Pat M'Durmer said he always came 'widin a flip av winnin','
An' his sire had come from England, 'n' his dam was from the States.

Friends would argue with M'Durmer, and they said he was in error
To put up his horse the Screamer, for he'd lose in any case,
And they said a city racer by the name of Holy Terror
Was regarded as the winner of the coming steeplechase;
But he said he had the knowledge to come in when it was raining,
And irrelevantly mentioned that he knew the time of day,
So he rose in their opinion. It was noticed that the training
Of the Screamer was conducted in a dark, mysterious way.

Well, the day arrived in glory; 'twas a day of jubilation
With careless-hearted bushmen for a hundred miles around,
An' the rum 'n' beer 'n' whisky came in waggons from the station,
An' the Holy Terror talent were the first upon the ground.
Judge M'Ard—with whose opinion it was scarcely safe to wrestle—
Took his dangerous position on the bark-and-sapling stand:
He was what the local Stiggins used to speak of as a 'wessel
'Of wrath,' and he'd a bludgeon that he carried in his hand.

'Off ye go!' the starter shouted, as down fell a stupid jockey—
Off they started in disorder—left the jockey where he lay—
And they fell and rolled and galloped down the crooked course and rocky,
Till the pumping of the Screamer could be heard a mile away.
But he kept his legs and galloped; he was used to rugged courses,

And he lumbered down the gully till the ridge began to quake:
And he ploughed along the siding, raising earth till other horses
An' their riders, too, were blinded by the dust-cloud in his wake.

From the ruck he'd struggled slowly—they were much surprised to find him
Close abeam of Holy Terror as along the flat they tore—
Even higher still and denser rose the cloud of dust behind him,
While in more divided splinters flew the shattered rails before.
'Terror!' 'Dead heat!' they were shouting—'Terror!' but the Screamer hung out
Nose to nose with Holy Terror as across the creek they swung,
An' M'Durmer shouted loudly, 'Put yer tongue out! put yer tongue out!'
An' the Screamer put his tongue out, and he won by half-a-tongue.

BUT WHAT'S THE USE

BUT what's the use of writing 'bush'—
Though editors demand it—
For city folk, and farming folk,
Can never understand it.
They're blind to what the bushman sees
The best with eyes shut tightest,
Out where the sun is hottest and
The stars are most and brightest.

The crows at sunrise flopping round
Where some poor life has run down;
The pair of emus trotting from
The lonely tank at sundown,
Their snaky heads well up, and eyes
Well out for man's manœuvres,
And feathers bobbing round behind
Like fringes round improvers.

The swagman tramping 'cross the plain;
Good Lord, there's nothing sadder,
Except the dog that slopes behind
His master like a shadder;
The turkey-tail to scare the flies,
The water-bag and billy;
The nose-bag getting cruel light,
The traveller getting silly.

The plain that seems to Jackaroos
Like gently sloping rises,
The shrubs and tufts that's miles away
But magnified in sizes;
The track that seems arisen up
Or else seems gently slopin',
And just a hint of kangaroos
Way out across the open.

The joy and hope the swagman feels
Returning, after shearing,
Or after six months' tramp Out Back,
He strikes the final clearing.
His weary spirit breathes again,

His aching legs seem limber
When to the East across the plain
He spots the Darling Timber!

But what's the use of writing 'bush'—
Though editors demand it—
For city folk and cockatoos,
They do not understand it.
They're blind to what the whaler sees
The best with eyes shut tightest,
Out where Australia's widest, and
The stars are most and brightest.

                                                    MAY, 1902.

Milton Keynes UK
Ingram Content Group UK Ltd.
UKHW042145281024
450365UK00010B/636